FRENCH HATS
IN IRAN

HEYDAR RADJAVI

Mage Publishers
Washington DC

LIBRARY OF CONGRESS CATALOGING-IN-PUBLICATION DATA
Radjavi, Heydar.
French hats in Iran / Heydar Radjavi.
   p. cm.
ISBN-13: 978-1-933823-45-4 (hardcover : alk. paper)
ISBN-10: 1-933823-45-3 (hardcover : alk. paper)
1. Radjavi, Heydar--Childhood and youth. 2. Radjavi, Heydar-
-Family. 3. Tabriz (Iran)--Biography. 4. Tabriz (Iran)--Social
life and customs--20th century. 5. Social change--Iran--Tabriz--
History--20th century. I. Title.
DS325.T14R23 2011
955'.3--dc22
[B]
                                                    2010042124

MAGE PUBLISHERS
WASHINGTON, DC
202-342-1642 • 800-962-0922
AS@MAGE.COM
VISIT MAGE ONLINE AT WWW.MAGE.COM

They have removed our hats.
An Iranian way of saying "We have been cheated."

They have put hats on our heads.
Another Iranian way of saying "We have been cheated."

CONTENTS

PREFACE 9

HANG ON TO YOUR WIGS 13

THE SCHOOL UNIFORM 27

THE SECOND LIFE OF A TAMBOURINE 35

MY FATHER'S WARDROBE 47

BODIES AND SOULS REPAIRED NEXT DOOR . . . 53

FATHER NEEDS PROOF. 67

HALVAH FROM UNRIPE GRAPES 73

INK FOR LIFE 83

NO LONGER IMPOLITE TO CHEW GUM 91

THE ARDUOUS PATH TO MY FIRST MOVIE . . . 99

GOOD SONGS, EVIL SONGS 115

GET A CHAPEAU AND A DIPLOMA 131

MY TEACHER'S SCANDALOUS TRANSFORMATION . 141

ARTS AND SCIENCES MADE EASY 157

OUR TEACHER WAS UNDER-APPRECIATED . . . 167

CREAM PUFFS AND A BLUE SUIT 177

MY SINGLE DAY IN MILITARY SERVICE 185

THE PSEUDONYMOUS COLUMNIST 197

PREFACE

THESE ARE SKETCHES OF LIFE in twentieth-century Iran, a nation in ambivalent flirtation with modernity for the past hundred years. The inevitable clashes with traditional beliefs, customs, and attitudes, at once comical and cruel, were experienced and are now reported in the following pages by one witness, this author, mainly through his childhood and adolescence.

Frangi hats arrived in Iran half a decade before World War Two started. The ruling monarch at the time, Reza Shah, the father of the last Shah of Iran, must have considered this event as the culmination of his efforts in forced Westernization of his subjects. Dress reforms had been introduced earlier, but it was at this time that the old Shah ordered the nation to go all the way: any woman who ventured out of her house had to bare her face; any man or woman insisting on a head-cover had to wear one of the two prescribed types of these new "French" hats.

Although the word Frangi can be translated as "French," it has, for several centuries, had a much wider application for Iranians. It simply means anybody or anything European or

Western. The Shah's compulsory dress codes, seen by their stubborn advocates as an important ingredient of modernization and progress, and thus well worth the pain, proved extremely unpopular with traditionalists. The reforms and their consequences strongly colored the early lives of my generation among ordinary city-dwellers of Tabriz, as the stories attest. Frangi hats appear literally in several of the narratives that follow, and can be viewed as symbolically present in virtually all of them.

Absolute accuracy in the narration cannot be guaranteed, of course. Pitfalls of memory, those unconscious revisions of personal history, are among obvious excuses for this, but there are others. Names of some main characters, ordinary folks who could not be remembered kindly, have been altered to prevent ready identification by their offspring. (The characters themselves, if still alive and able to read these reports from long ago and far away, will have no problem recognizing themselves.) Furthermore, some secondary characters with indistinguishable roles have at times been combined to keep the population under control.

I have introduced non-English words only when really necessary. My transliteration of names of people and places may not always be consistent with those the reader sees in the daily news. What may seem even worse is that a few words appear with more than one spelling. This was necessitated by my attempt to be as faithful as possible to the pronunciation in the local tongue. The all-important word "Frangi" introduced above is an example: it represents the pronunciation in Tabriz; the reader may have encountered it in such other forms as "Farangi" or "Ferangee."

Each piece is meant to be read independently; so I hope the reader doesn't mind an occasional reminder of a fact, an event, or a character already met in another story. One small warning: in the face of the current extreme violence engulfing that troubled region of the world, some readers might find the contents unfashionably, and perhaps idiotically, light-hearted. I have no excuses to offer. May light hearts reign once again.

HANG ON TO YOUR WIGS

I HAD JUST FINISHED MY FIRST DELICIOUS PIECE of pastry at the big wedding party for women and children attended by my mother and me. I was sitting politely next to Mother and behaving myself, in anticipation of more goodies to be offered by the hostesses. I was admiring the huge dishes filled with cakes and candies on the table on the far side of the elaborately decorated guest room when I heard a sudden loud cry from the adjoining small room. That was where the bride was being prepared for the ceremony. I left the party room into which more women and children, dressed in their best party clothes, were still being ushered, and ran toward the source of the cry. It was the bride, nine-year-old Afshan, who had, under the stern and embarrassed gazes of her mother and grandmother, stopped crying aloud now but was still sobbing incessantly. Until a couple of months earlier, she had played with me and a few other children almost every week, while her mother and mine, long-time close friends, exchanged visits. We, the younger kids, loved this pretty and happy playmate, who was always ready to lend us her toys. I had never seen her cry before, which made me believe that kids didn't cry when they reached her age.

The reason for Afshan's crying was not her reluctance to marry the fourteen-year-old neighbor boy whose family together with hers had negotiated the match. She wouldn't think of disobeying her father, and she wasn't in a position to appreciate the enormity of the step that was being taken for her. But the idea of separation from her lovely Persian cat was something she was not yet ready to accept. She was standing in her wedding gown, holding the cat in her arms as tightly as she could, weeping and protesting. Her mother was trying to pry the cat out of her embrace in preparation for the marriage ritual. "You can come back home every day, dear, and visit the cat," she kept saying. The groom's household, which would be Afshan's home at dusk this day, did not allow pet cats. They were a nuisance, the groom's father had said, and they interfered with the clean setting required for his daily prayers. This was an extreme view; many very religious people, including Afshan's parents, had no problems with cats so long as they were trained and didn't shed too much hair. The faithful just had to make sure that their praying garments were free of cat hair.

Afshan's grooming for the duties of adult life had commenced as soon as she turned nine, the age of "female responsibility." The corresponding male age of fourteen was still very safely far in the future for me and the other boys among Afshan's playmates. We had first viewed it with considerable amusement that Afshan's dress code was now identical to that of the grownups. The miniature adult, too, seemed delighted for a while; she was playing dress-up in a big way. But things started to change soon. Her socialization time with the kids was curtailed while her home tutoring for adulthood was given priority. At first, we missed her terribly at our games. Then we started to get used to the idea. When the news of her engagement and imminent wedding came, it wasn't so much a shock as a relief to us: we were healed by what would decades later be rediscovered as a best-selling goal of therapy and termed "closure" thereafter.

Now I was transfixed in the corner of this room with disbelief: Afshan the bride, an adult by definition, was acting like a child. I didn't have much time to contemplate the mystery. My presence in the small preparation room, once noticed, was strongly discouraged. So I went to the court-yard to play with the other little boys and girls, all young enough not only to be allowed to play with the members of the opposite sex, but also to come and go freely between the men's and women's separate guest rooms. The latter was by far the larger of the two. A wedding party in the urban part of Tabriz had almost always been primarily a women's affair. On this day, my father was among ten or fifteen close friends of the family who were attending the subdued male reception, which had started earlier than the women's and would end long before most of the women arrived. My mother and I were among the early arrivals, those relatives and friends in the innermost circle having the privilege of participation in the wedding rituals, before the more public celebrations began.

The marriage was illegal. The bride and groom would have to wait several years before their marriage could be registered officially at the Bureau of Vital Statistics. The parents didn't care, so long as the required religious rites were observed. Meanwhile, the Bureau officials, as well as the law enforcement folks, were powerless: how could they possibly object to kids' sleep-overs among neighbors?

By the time the presiding clergyman, needed for sanctifying the marriage, arrived, Afshan and her entourage had been moved from the small room into the women's guest room and seated next to the curtain that separated the two rooms. The clergyman, after a brief meeting with the men on the other side of the courtyard, was led to the small room, where he was served tea and sweets. He was unable to see any of the female guests; so the women did not have to cover themselves individually. At the auspicious moment, which had already been determined by an expert perusal of the movements of heavenly bodies, he recited appropriate passages from the Holy Scriptures and asked the ritual question. I was watching Afshan who now looked more like a decorated doll than her old little self. Her dress was beautiful and her heavily made-up face was tear-free. She was wearing a crown made of fine artificial flowers, illuminated by numerous tiny colored light bulbs. She had been duly coached: she knew that the clergyman's loud and clear question coming from the other side of the curtain should be ignored twice. Thus after the third prompting she consented to the marriage proposal, uttering a barely audible "yes" with rehearsed adult dignity. Three "innocent" boys, including me, were given three rings to place on her fingers, in the order dictated by the proximity of each boy's parents to the wedding families.

I missed the ritual at the men's quarters, but I concluded from what Mother told me that it was quite boring. It was dominated by the signing of the necessary sacred documents. Nobody put a ring on the groom's fingers at the ceremony. As I would learn later during similar events, the groom just sat there, nervously watched the older and wiser men, and spoke only when spoken to. He was not to see the bride until late that night, after she had been delivered to his home and after the wedding celebrations in the new home had come to an end. A family would have had to be more "modern" to allow the guests, the female guests only of course, a glimpse of the bride and groom together. Very few of the guests at this party were that modern, although most of them would opine, in private, that wedding nine-year-olds to fourteen-year-olds was overdoing it a bit. The Government's minimum age was unrealistic, they were sure, but it wouldn't hurt to wait three or four more years.

As soon as the men left the house, it was time for music and dancing. At almost all the weddings I had attended with my mother before, professional female musicians were the main attraction. Even religious men, who would normally prohibit music in their households, looked the other way on a wedding occasion, and let their women have their way. The master of this household, however, being more religious than most, even on this rare occasion would only allow one approved instrument, called *tabla gaval.* The second word stood for a very common, tambourine-like, instrument. The first, the adjective, indicated the modification necessary to make it permissible: no jingling bells around it to make its possession and use sinful. "A gaval with all its teeth pulled out," a women whispered to another when it became clear that all the wedding party was going to get was two amateurs playing tabla gavals. The young women present had not expected professional musicians, considered evil by Afshan's father. But they had hoped for real gavals played by skilled guests. Skilled players of real gavals wouldn't touch the primitive, toothless instrument.

Now that the house was the women's and kids' alone, a torrent of female guests was pouring in. They were all wearing the best dresses and finest jewelry they owned or could make, buy, or borrow for the occasion, revealed only after they were safely inside the house. To avoid the sin of exposing their natural and artificial beauty to the strange men in the street, almost all of them were, until they stepped inside, covered by modest overalls and real or improvised, in some cases ridiculous-looking, hats.

The preferred outerwear for most of the female guests was of course not the long and loose coat they were wearing, but a *charshub*, a head-to-toe black shroud which would leave only their eyes and part of their faces uncovered. But there was a big problem with this: five or six years earlier, Reza Shah, the ruling monarch of Iran, had decided to extend his modernization programs from the male to the female population of the country. The initial methods of persuasion and benign coercion had not worked. The Shah would now emancipate the women of Iran, for their own good, at any cost. Policemen patrolling the streets were ordered to stop any women reluctant to modernize, and tear their charshubs and head-scarves into pieces on the spot. These men, to whom my pious neighbors referred, in private, as "agents of corruption" or "immorality police" went easy on the scarves in wintertime, but would not otherwise tolerate anything but a hat. Completely bare hair, an alternative unthinkable to the faithful, was of course permitted by the police.

There were occasional well-dressed women in agreement with the new dress codes whom I saw in some Tabriz streets, wearing fitting coats and fashionable *Frangi* hats or an exposed hairdo. Orthodox men diverted their eyes when they met a willingly modern woman, said a short prayer, and sometimes uttered a mild, almost inaudible, curse to Satan. The women of orthodox men simply stayed home unless it was absolutely necessary to venture out, mainly to run to the neighborhood public bath-house once a week. Those few who could afford it, had a little bath-house built in their homes, a major feat for that time and place. A rich, charity-minded neighbor of ours, constructed a bath-house spacious and comfortable enough to accommodate not only his large family, but also the desperate neighbor women whenever the dreaded emancipation cops patrolling our streets were reported to be especially vicious.

The pious women hid their charshubs in their closets and saved them. They were certain that, some day, they would be able to use the garments again. This was only a minor inconvenience, they believed, a device of the Almighty to test the strength of their faith. The old Shah's tyranny would come to an end, they said, God willing, and the forces of decency would once again prevail.

But the overwhelming majority of women did not want to stay home. They started to use various, sometimes ingenious, tricks to protect their modesty and honor. A common solution, one that we had resorted to on this wedding day, for example, was bribing the immorality police.

My grown-up brother accompanied my mother and me to the bride's house and pleaded with the inescapable roving agent of modernization to let Mother keep her scarf on account of a bad cold. The young cop, after making sure that no superior was watching him from a distance, gracefully accepted a little "tea money" offered in appreciation of the understanding that he was about to show.

Among the women now arriving at the party, there was a very conspicuous one whom I had seen only once or twice before, and whom I would never forget. She was Afshan's aunt. The other women, most of them never having been permitted to go to school, thought of her as "the literate woman." She lived in Tabriz, but did not socialize much with the bride's family. On the wedding day, she was even more elegantly dressed than I remembered, but what made her really stand out was that she had no hat on, very unusual for the neighborhood. Heads turned her way when she passed through the gate, some in curiosity and disbelief and some in awe and envy. But then something happened that was no less than a miracle to me. She went to the coat room and removed not only her overcoat, but also, what seemed to me her entire hair. Not knowing anything about hair-pieces, I expected to see the bare skin of her head. But underneath the neat wig was her own hair which, I thought, was almost identical to the outer layer, only slightly less puffy. An old woman let out a sigh of relief, upon learning that the new arrival's virtue was intact after all, albeit by resorting to a questionable method.

The miraculous device, the object of my curiosity for long afterward, was questionable indeed. In the few months' time that was left of the ruling Shah's own life on the throne, God-fearing women and men would be heard arguing about whether a man glancing at a woman wearing "artificial hair" was committing a sin anyway, if he assumed the hair to be real. The questions were numerous and complex: What about the wig-wearing women themselves, for instance? True that they deceived the immorality police and the stubborn Shah, but weren't they, like Satan's own loyal accomplices, also deceiving strange men? What if an evil modern woman was actually showing her own hair in public, only pretending when faced with virtuous relatives, that it was a wig?

The wigged woman kissed her niece good-bye and left before the groom's party arrived to "take the bride home." It was fortunate that the two families were neighbors; otherwise, they would have to deal with the problem posed by the custom of transporting the bride and her entourage, now doubled in size, by horse-driven carriages. Such a spectacle in Tabriz streets would certainly attract a multitude of emancipation agents, not all susceptible to bribes. Mother and I, like most of the bride's party, weren't invited to the groom's house. We said our farewells and left the house as Afshan was being transferred. My brother was waiting at the door to escort Mother and me back home, with enough change in his pocket for potentially understanding cops' tea money. As we were exiting the cul-de-sac containing Afshan's old and new homes, a large sheep was being sacrificed at the gate of the new home to welcome the bride.

The prayers by the faithful, who had anxiously waited so long to get those charshubs out of their closets and feel free and dignified again, were answered in a curious way. Tabriz was occupied by the Russians (and the whole country by one or other of the Allies in World War Two). The Shah, so bent on emancipation, was forced to abdicate his throne and leave the country. The new Shah was still too young and the new government too weak and too preoccupied with problems like food shortages to promote either morality or immorality. The day after the occupation, Saria Khanum, my best friend's grandmother and the most pious old woman in my neighborhood, put on her very special charshub and, braving the unsafe streets of a city in turmoil, went to visit like-minded friends. What made Saria Khanum's charshub special was the added "pitcha," which was despised even by my religious mother and considered a relic of the past century. This was a rectangular black screen, made of goat hair, for her to see through; no strange man, or woman for that matter, could see any part of her face through it. Saria Khanum immensely enjoyed her recaptured sense of freedom after six years of voluntary house arrest, and wondered why not all the women were celebrating. "May God grant the new Shah a long life," she prayed. The godly young Shah had, according to her, "learned from the terrible fate of his evil father and decided to choose the right path – God be praised a hundred thousand times."

I would never see Afshan's full face again. World War Two and the occupation ended. Through this and many ensuing social upheavals, Afshan observed the strict rules and regulations of her new, exceedingly conservative household. The undisputed master there, her father-in-law, did not allow the pretty bride out of the house, except for escorted visits to the bath-house and regular monthly visits to her parents living practically next door. His strict rules remained in force even after the immorality police were long gone. "The evil influences are always out there," he said when Afshan's mother pleaded with him to consider a parole for Afshan to attend the wedding of a former female playmate. The master and his son the groom, too, dug out their old traditional garments and hats, now that the Western dress codes, compulsory under the old Shah's rule, had become optional. Every weekday, the two of them came home directly as soon as they closed the doors of their stationery store in the bazaar, "a prosperous business by the grace of God." The son quit school after eighth grade by the master's order and concentrated on his role as a partner and heir apparent. They entertained only a small, prescreened set of friends and relatives at home.

The groom did not rebel as long as his father lived, and the posthumous rebellion was mild. When he had reached the approximate age of twenty-five, the son sold the store in the bazaar and moved to a "brighter, airier location" in a fashionable district. He expanded his business and stocked books and newspapers in the store, where my school friends and I often went to browse. He threw away his traditional clothes and donned a Western suit, but no tie. He decided that his daughter, and not just his son, should attend school. "These are different times," he said, quoting a revered Founding Father of the Faith, "and different times require different rules." The times were not different enough for Afshan, however, to expose her face in public. But she freely attended wedding parties and other gatherings in sufficiently pious households, including mine. There was no question that their son should finish high school. They had debates on whether their daughter should start high school or just wait to get married. While the daughter was still in third or fourth grade, I once saw her in her dad's store. It had been about fifteen years since her parents' marriage. She was in her school uniform and wore no head scarf. I asked her if she had a cat. Yes, she said, and she had four kittens besides. I chatted with the father a bit. I inquired about his family. He did not blush or show any sign of discomfort when I mentioned Afshan by name. His father, like mine, would not have allowed such indiscretions. "How is the home?" he would have expected me to ask. "The home is fine," his appropriate answer would have run, "and sends greetings. How is yours?"

I did have several occasions to see the modern aunt with the miraculous wig. Both she and my mother assured me and other skeptics that, in spite of their own initial natural misgivings, Afshan's marriage had turned out to be a very happy one. I last saw the aunt, together with Afshan's grown family, in my mother's house. Afshan's mother and mother-in-law were also present. Thirty-some years had passed since that memorable wedding, and it was a treat to watch the four generations, so different in their outlooks, in seeming harmony of sorts. The aunt was old now, but as beautiful, and as elegantly dressed, as she had been at the wedding so long ago. Her hair, or was it her hair-piece, had turned white. I didn't want to find out; I preferred to enjoy the delicious mystery of whether one was committing a sin by admiring her neat hairdo. Afshan's mother and mother-in-law were wearing charshubs when they entered the house, which they kept on, because of my presence. They covered their faces except for their eyes, exchanged brief pleasantries with me, but talked mainly to women. They would feel much more comfortable without a man in the room, of course. Afshan was wearing a light-colored flowery *chadra* (not one of those black charshubs) over her undoubtedly fashionable dress, covering all of her hair but revealing most of her face. The exposure of the rest of her face, all of her hair, and her dress would have to wait until there was no man in the room.

Afshan's son, a doctor of medicine, was wearing a suit and a tie. Her daughter, with flowing hair that was clearly not "artificial," was in a thoroughly modern dress. She was a school teacher, married and with two children of her own. The older child, a very cheerful and lively girl, had been brought along. Her mother was obviously very pleased with her accomplishments in school and described them to me in detail. "Tell him what else she is doing," said the aunt mischievously. "Yes, she is also very musical, and she likes acting," said the proud mother, "and she is enrolled in Madam Nazarian's Music School." I exchanged glances with Afshan's husband. His face assumed a dark look for a fleeting moment. "My late father would have spat on my face for this," he said. "And my father on mine," said Afshan, and they both laughed. "Different times, different rules" he said, to everyone's approval.

Half a century after Afshan was so abruptly and prematurely catapulted to the adult world, and thirteen years after the most recent revolution in Iran, I visited my relatives and friends in Tehran. Different times, different rules, again.

I had been away for a long time. But just as it had been the case so long ago, the new rules applied only out-doors. At a dinner party I attended, the female guests arrived in one of the few officially approved forms of outerwear, exposing no more than their faces and hands. As soon as each woman arrived, however, she assumed her preferred image. Some of the women retained their head-gear on account of the mixed company. Some bared their heads, revealed their trendy minis and maxis, and let the men decide whether or not to cast sinful eyes on them. Many of them, however, turned out to be conservatively dressed when they took off what they called their outer uniforms. I counted as many bare heads as properly sin-proofed ones now that, in the safety of a home, everybody was free to choose.

A guest recommended a live play he had recently seen, put on by an excellent company, he said. Among the main performers' names he mentioned, I thought I recognized Afshan's grand-daughter's. This wasn't surprising, of course, but something else was: the play was a Western piece in translation, with very substantial parts for women, which necessitated for them to bare their hair. "How is it possible," I asked the guest, "now that ever-present morality police are watching every move of every woman in the street?" His own wife had been stopped and reprimanded by the cruising agents of decency just a few days earlier, her infraction being that an inch of her hair was inadvertently showing. A woman overheard me and was especially amused by my naïveté. "The theater folks are very resourceful," she said. "If you read the program notes carefully, you'll be informed that, to avoid sinful exposure, the female actors wear wigs."

THE SCHOOL UNIFORM

MANY MONTHS BEFORE I STARTED ELEMENTARY SCHOOL, I was promised my first tailor-made piece of clothing, a regulation suit for all elementary schools in Iran at the time. I could hardly wait for that status symbol I so admired on the older kids in the neighborhood. Ready-made clothing was unheard of, and everybody's dresses and suits had to be made at home or by a tailor. Acquiring an item of clothing was an infrequent but major operation. It included shopping for material, comparing prices, and long discussions with friends and neighbors: Was English-made woolen material really worth its exorbitant price? Didn't the cheaper Japanese version last just about as long? Or should one go with domestically made material, and save enough for a second suit? Then there was the problem of finding out whether that coveted phrase sewn onto the margin of the material, "Made in England," was genuine. If not, even the claim that the material was one hundred percent wool was of course suspect, and there were tests available to verify it. My father always insisted on burning a tiny piece of the material he was considering: nothing, he believed, would burn or smoke like real wool.

In the case of six-year-old boys, the procedure was simplified a lot by the federal school regulations. There were only two types of material allowed for school uniforms, one for boys and one for girls. They were both manufactured domestically, for economic and patriotic reasons. You just purchased it at any material store, of course after the tailor had measured the customer and determined how much was needed. The matter of whether to trust the tailor didn't come up in a kid's case. Adult customers usually memorized the amount of cloth needed for each garment, to prevent potentially unscrupulous tailors from stealing enough remnants to make a hat they could sell on the sly. My older brother always demanded, as part of his negotiations with a prospective tailor for his new suit, that a matching hat be thrown in, although the material was just deemed sufficient for the suit. Matching *kepis* were all the rage among cool young men around twenty years of age.

After two or three visits I made to the tailor shop, accompanied by my brother, the project was completed. My brother did not negotiate for a matching hat from the remnants. For one thing, the school regulations required a special type of hat called *casquette*. These resembled the military hats that had adorned the heads of departed Russian czars (as I had seen on the pre-revolution Russian bank-notes, now useless and thus available for us kids to play with) and were made only in special hat shops. My uniform was ready to wear a month before I would start school, putting me in a constant state of excited anticipation.

Nine days before school started, World War Two came to Tabriz. A few days of turmoil were followed by a long occupation. It took three weeks for the all-powerful Shah to abdicate officially, but all his modernizing and secularizing powers, for which he was so terribly feared, had evaporated in the first hours of occupation. Traditional citizens of Tabriz saw it all as divine intervention. "Hadn't the old Shah been asking for it for years?" they put to each other, and to anyone who listened. Then they nodded knowingly, feeling liberated and showing it. Gone were the Shah's strict dress codes. Every pious man threw away his compulsory *Frangi* suit and hat, let his beard grow, and slipped into his comfortable, old-fashioned robe. Every pious woman once again donned her stowed-away *charshub*, the black tent-like apparel that, when properly wrapped, hid everything except her eyes from the potentially sinful male glances.

The War changed more than just the dress codes. Suddenly, I began to hear a lot about how things were getting scarce and expensive, and how everybody was getting poorer. (It was only later that I learned some people were getting much, much richer.) Everyday needs were now being rationed. Long bread lines formed at subsidized bakeries. The price of tea, an absolutely essential requirement at an Iranian breakfast, before and after every meal or snack, the only drink other than sweetened, diluted fruit juice in summertime that many families ever knew, became prohibitive. "It is God's punishment for all of us, not just the infidel Shah," maintained my next-door neighbor, known to many as Lady Saria, the Pious. "We are all responsible," she said to my mother, "for going along with whatever ungodly policy the Shah introduced; we must suffer now." But Lady Saria missed her tea terribly. So when my mother learned, I don't remember from whom, that a tea substitute could be made with sun-dried apple peels, Saria was ready to help Mother with the production of poor man's tea. She was even willing to forgo a few of her beloved religious mourning sessions, now legal and above-ground again, thanks to the departure of the sinful Shah. The small apples from the trees in our courtyard had never proved so valuable. We were even able to supply a few neighbors with the new tea. Then sugar also got scarce. We started to save our small monthly ration of sugar for our guests' tea. With our own tea, we used raisins, still available in the local market.

A lot of things changed in the neighborhood, but not the school kids' uniform. Some old folks made noises about that too. Wasn't this school uniform also a manifestation of the Shah's mindless surrender to *Frangi* ways? they asked. But their cries were ignored even by the faithful, too poor to throw away their kids' perfectly good, harmless outfits. So when the school opened, all of us new pupils proudly wore our new uniforms. None of our teachers had changed their appearance either; they all still had their western suits and ties on. In girls' schools too, as I learned from the neighbor girls, there were no changes in their teachers' dresses, at least while in school, at least for now.

My first uniform was also my last tailor-made one in elementary school. For the next five years my mother saved money by personally tailoring my school uniforms, one per year. Most of my friends' mothers did the same, but we kids totally avoided conversations on this delicate matter. Prices on everything kept rising. Even some ordinary spices became luxury items. One explanation I would hear for the high price of pepper was that it was an ingredient for the kind of bombs that were just tested in Japan.

When I started secondary school after the War, my father resumed the annual custom of having a school uniform made for me by the neighborhood tailor. A year later, when I was given my second secondary school uniform, I decided to use it sparingly for a while; there were school functions to attend on weekends, and it would be nice to be spiffy for those occasions. New Year's Day was coming in six months' time, which required a new-looking, if not new, outfit. So I said yes to Mother's offer of turning my old uniform inside out.

Having made my uniforms single-handedly for the five years in elementary school, she felt confident that she would do an expert job. "Nobody will be able to tell," she said. The embarrassment of being found out, she knew, could be painful. She herself had to resist the temptation to buy one of those "like-new" garments that had flooded the market just after the War. These were used American clothing items, no doubt donated to charities initially, that had somehow found their way into the local bazaar. They were very affordable, but wearing them was tantamount to confession of poverty. Their American shapes and styles were unmistakable, and it was impossible to pretend that they were home-made or domestically tailored.

A recent experience had bolstered my trust in Mother's skills. On that occasion, she succeeded in making a nice jacket for me to wear at a wedding: she actually purchased a used American coat from the farthest reaches of the bazaar. She didn't let me accompany her, to make sure that nobody would recognize her in the act. Not that she was very recognizable in her charshub, but it didn't hurt to be on the safe side. When she brought the garment home, she took it apart, cut several large panels of fabric out of it to be used for the jacket, and threw the rest in the rag basket. She decided that, of her two favorite dyeing agents, onion skins and dried pomegranate peels, the latter would give better results. She dyed the material with the peels that she had saved for such occasions as this. Then she fashioned it into a very credible, absolutely new-looking party jacket for me.

Thus it was that I looked forward to seeing the result of Mother's promised inversion operation on my old school uniform. I watched her undo the whole garment, then put the pieces together on the reverse side, carefully following the original seams. She transformed it. What had looked drab, dusty, and weather-beaten, now shined with fresh life. It even smelled like a new garment.

It was a happy morning when I wore the inverted uniform for the first time. The luxury of having a choice of two uniforms was intoxicating. I felt rich as I took a languid walk to school, a joyful promenade. My very rich classmate, Farhad, the Governor General's son, arrived in the chauffeur-driven family car as I was entering the school yard, just in time for the first class of the morning. He was in one of his many nice uniforms. "I hate all my school uniforms," he had said many times before, "they are so shapeless and so confining." He was thankful that he could change to "reasonable" clothes after school and when he went to parties or entertained friends at home. But here, in the school yard, where nobody could wear anything else before twelfth grade, I was now Farhad's equal of sorts – thanks to the combined efforts of Mother and the Ministry of Education.

The feeling of opulence was short-lived. As soon as I arrived in the classroom and took my designated place next to my bench-mate, he whispered his congratulations on an inversion job well done. For a moment, I considered a categorical denial, but he saved me half the double embarrassment. "I can easily tell," he said, supplying me with irrefutable proof, "because your breast pocket has moved from left to right."

"YOU CAN HAVE THE GOAT EXCEPT FOR THE SKIN" said Mother to the old woman who came to collect the creature that I had considered my pet for the past few months. I was sad but not shocked. I even knew what Mother intended to do with the skin. I had been prepared for this eventuality since that spring day, when the baby goat arrived. A farmer, who owed Father a favor, had delivered it to our backyard as a "gift for the little one." This was just a polite code, supposed to imply that the offering wasn't worthy of the master of the house. The farmer's assumption, made clear to me by Father as soon as the farmer left, was that the animal would be slaughtered shortly for the household consumption. Father was not very pleased with the gift: he was no vegetarian, but he had never directly ordered an animal's demise except for the one time during his obligatory pilgrimage to Mecca, when he could not bend God's explicit rule that demanded the ceremonial sacrifice of a lamb.

There were no municipal regulations against keeping animals, big or small, in back or front yards. We always had half a dozen chickens that supplied us with all the eggs we needed. We had what would be called, decades later in health-food documentaries, a "free-range chicken environment." The cute black goat joined the environment and was loved by all the kids on the block. It was only tolerated by the grownups as long as it was tiny. But when its horns started to look substantial, Father said it was becoming dangerous. I did not expect to be consulted in the matter. "We can use the meat," said Mother. "No," said Father, "just give the goat to Hava." Hava was the old woman who did our weekly laundry to supplement her husband's meager income. She was also my baby-sitter on the rare occasions Mother had to go somewhere without me. (To my taste, these occasions were becoming too frequent; some wedding invitations were starting to be more explicit in forbidding the accompaniment of children.)

There was no way out now, and everyone knew it. I was resigned to the inevitability: at the end of the summer, my pet was going to end up in Hava's little kitchen. Hava and her husband were very happy to hear the news. This was probably one of the more valuable gifts they had ever received – thanks more to Father's peculiarity than to his generosity. Mother attached a string to the gift, however: the skin was to be returned to her without Father's knowledge. Mother and I had a secret, and she knew that I would not betray it to Father. In fact, the secret helped me overcome the pain caused by the imminent loss of my pet. The skin would live on in the form of a musical instrument resembling a large tambourine, called *gaval* in the local tongue, into which Mother would fashion it. I was already quite familiar with the bitter-sweet history of the underground existence of music in the household.

Father was against all "adult" musical instruments. Musical toys for kids were only frowned upon by him, but all real "instruments of frivolity" were strictly forbidden. The ban didn't quite work, of course. Mother, who was much younger than Father, was religious but did not consider music sinful. Thanks to Father's regular working habits, Mother always knew what time he would arrive home on weekdays. So at some of her afternoon, after-chores get-togethers with the neighbor women, of all age groups, she would ask them to bring along their gavals, the most common and least costly instruments available. The other kids and I enjoyed these musical events, often accompanied by cakes and candies, at least as much as the adults did. It was only during the holy mourning months of the lunar year that these sessions were entirely abandoned.

Nearly all of the husbands on the block were younger and less strict than Father. My "Aunt" Rubi, known for what the neighbors called her postal-card beauty, lived next door. A young bride, whose elaborate wedding I had attended with Mother about a year earlier, Rubi was an accomplished gaval player. Her husband, a starting clerk in the local branch of the Government Bureau of Vital Statistics, didn't just condone her gaval playing; he enjoyed it. He even sang with her in the privacy of their home. I could hear them through the little opening, high in the wall that separated our kitchen from theirs. They never played or sang in the evening when Father, the oldest and wisest man of the neighborhood, was around and could hear them. Rubi was the toast of the afternoon tea parties for women and children. No grown man was allowed to see or hear her play; that would be sinful by the uniform standards of the neighborhood. We little boys, too, would soon outlive our privileged years of innocence and lose our passports into mixed company.

I would forever remember one of the very few occasions on which Father came home unexpectedly early, no doubt for some very good reason, disrupting a frivolous afternoon tea party. It was a beautiful day, the kind of summer day that made Tabriz a tourist destination for those inhabitants of the hot cities of Iran who could afford to know the meaning of "tourist." The quadrangle that formed the protected front yard of our house looked lovely with its mulberry and plum trees and its central flower and vegetable garden. The courtyard of every house in large cities like Tabriz was, by millennia-old tradition, surrounded by high walls to ensure security and privacy. No master of a household worthy of his title would permit strangers to catch a glimpse of the womenfolk working or playing freely in the yard.

Our quadrangle was, except for the small backyard in one corner, bordered by the neighbors' houses on all the four sides, making it extra secure. It also made direct and easy access to the street impossible. This wasn't an uncommon occurrence in the maze of traditional Tabriz houses, and the builders of our particular neighborhood had known how to deal with the problem. They had built, a century and a half before my time, a long, narrow, almost underground, corridor that led from the street entrance to the quadrangle. Thus it was difficult to hear the door knocker. Father wouldn't have anything to do with doorbells, which used electricity, "too dangerous" for a house to be equipped with. So we always reminded our prospective visitors to knock loudly. How grateful Mother and I would prove to be this summer afternoon for having as cumbersome an approach to the house as we did!

Several women, casually seated on the thick carpet that Mother had spread on the shady side of the courtyard for the occasion, were sipping tea and eating freshly-cut pieces of fruit. Aunt Rubi and two other women were playing their gavals and singing when the potential calamity occurred. There was a knock on the door, which Mother immediately recognized as Father's knock. I, too, would have recognized it, were I not distracted by the other kids in the yard. Father had a unique, hasty knock which I would, years later, identify as a "cha-cha-cha knock." Wartime feelings of insecurity still ran deep in Tabriz, so Father had trained us to use the two extra-long safety latches on the back of the main door every time somebody left the house. Thus even Father had to knock and wait for us to open the door from the inside. Mother instructed me to open the door and tell Father that there were women in the yard. "And don't run," she hastened to add.

Suitably warned, Father moved slowly through the corridor, so the adult female guests could have time to cover themselves properly, as expected. When he reached the front yard, the women, all covered in their *chadras* by now, rose to greet the embodiment of wisdom and piety that was Father. Fortunately, he was too modest to look in the direction of the three young women whose normally slim figures were bulging under their chadras, which now accommodated the large gavals also. Peace prevailed.

Father didn't allow a radio in the house, of course. (But, several years later, he wouldn't object to my building a little crystal earphone radio. That contraption, a great source of joy for me, would luckily and surprisingly pass as a toy.) Aunt Rubi had a real radio set, given to her by her father as a wedding gift. I often listened to music emanating from her miraculous set, sometimes directly while visiting her house and sometimes through the "window." The high opening between our back-to-back kitchens allowed Mother not only to enjoy the music while preparing meals, but also to give Rubi occasional hints on her recipes.

A cousin of mine, who had recently lost his father and left his childhood city of Istanbul for good, was living with us at the time and going through the last years of high school together with my older brother. Among his few prized possessions brought along from Istanbul were a winding phonograph and quite a few records of Turkish songs. Some days, when he came home from school, he would take the set out of his large trunk and treat us to the delightful recorded music. Then, before dusk, the regular time of Father's arrival at home, he would carefully gather together all the evidence and hide it again, deep within his trunk.

The unwritten pact of secrecy among the women and kids of the neighborhood was adhered to religiously, so to speak. Only a couple of their men were as strict as Father. Among the women neighbors, remarkably, only one came close: Saria Khanum, the pious. But she didn't go beyond advising the sinners and reminding them of their options. "Burn your instruments in this world," she would quote her favorite preacher with borrowed authority in her tone, but with absolutely no malice, "or you'll be burned yourselves in the next." Saria Khanum was of course not invited to the afternoon parties. She wouldn't go to useless parties anyway, with or without music. It should be said in fairness to her memory that she never tattled to the men about their women's activities.

The one squealer in my neighborhood's history, as far as I was aware, had come from my own family. My oldest male sibling, Kazem, by now a grown man over thirty, had done it when he was a little kid. He and my sister, Adalat, his senior by four years, were from Father's first wife, who was my mother's sister. After their mother's sudden death, the collective male wisdom of the extended family had dictated, in the interest of the orphaned children, that my father marry the deceased wife's sister. Hence the great age discrepancy between my parents.

Mother, seventeen at the time of her marriage, was just six years older than her niece Adalat, her new "daughter." A strong bond already existed between them, which would last for the rest of their lives. Among other things, they shared their love of music with a gaval that the teenage Adalat owned. This was a real gaval, an adult gaval, an upgraded gaval. Her toy gaval, overlooked by Father as long as she was a kid, had been discarded. This pleased Father. Little did he know that a replacement had been acquired through a trustworthy neighbor, who had a stationery shop next to a music store. This was the setting for the great betrayal by the little Kazem. The incident took place, after a fight between the siblings. The angry kid brother told Father about the secret gaval. The immediate consequence, as Mother related to me after those many years, was so terrible that just remembering it would diminish my guilt in every act of conspiracy ever undertaken by Mother and me against Father's excessive strictures. After making sure that the informer knew where the instrument of sin was hidden, the enraged father lent Kazem his pocket knife and bribed him to tear the gaval's delicate goatskin drum into little pieces.

Since the incident, Adalat had married and moved away. Kazem had become a teacher of Persian literature and considered himself as modern a man as any. He was no doubt repentant of his shameless childhood squealing. He had also moved away. But Mother, for some reason, hadn't until now acquired another gaval. Perhaps she didn't feel equal to the task of keeping it hidden without Adalat's help. Now my goat, soon to depart, provided the opportunity: old Hava took my former pet home with the promise of returning with the skin soon. Her husband, an underemployed handy-man, would slaughter the animal himself and do the skinning, chopping, and cutting. They would then cook the meat well with a lot of salt, and store it in fat for the coming winter.

Hava arrived at the door the day after the slaughter, in mid-morning to make sure Father wasn't home, and delivered the odorous skin. I am ashamed to report that the little gift Hava had for me completely cured any sorrow that I felt by associating the skin with its very recent contents. She handed me a "balloon."

The organic balloon, the bladder of the butchered goat, was the only kind of balloon I knew, with one exception: a neighbor girl's father had recently given her some

"American balloons." A few of us were having a lot of fun, one day, inflating these balloons and playing with them until another neighborhood father noticed us. "Just leave it to this stupid Hasan," he said furiously, referring to the little girl's father. "Give them to me, all of them," he ordered us, "I'll have to have a word with Hasan." He grabbed the lot, inflated and uninflated, and ran to Hasan's house. We followed him. "Where did you get these things, you idiot?" he demanded. Our confusion became total when he continued, "These are toys for adults, not kids!" Hasan was as confused as the kids, until the angry neighbor whispered a few words in his ear. Then Hasan apologetically explained that he had bought them in an American Army surplus sale. They came in large, sealed, wartime ration cans for soldiers. Each can contained snacks, instant coffee, orange juice powder, chewing gum and the like. Some also contained a couple of these toys in aluminum wrappings. "I can deal with the sinners," the angry father was now saying, addressing himself exclusively, "but God save us from the innocent." It was clear from the gravity of the air surrounding the incident that the kids shouldn't ask for a clarification. With this unpleasant and unexplained experience in mind, I was happy to receive the gift bladder, the more traditional balloon, which I knew would not cause a stir among the parents.

The smelly skin had to be processed by Mother now, but it couldn't be kept at home. Aunt Rubi and her husband had already agreed to keep it in their basement while Mother attended to it every day. I can't remember the details, but the process was not a short one. Nor do I know where and when Mother had learned to cure a goatskin. I do, however, remember with pleasure the day the skin, by then odorless and almost transparent, was brought home again. The old frame of Adalat's violated gaval, what Mother and I called the gaval's skeleton, had been kept intact for more than fifteen years. Having lost its capacity as an instrument of sin, it had coexisted peacefully with the other junk in our large basement. The frame, with all the little jingling bells around it, was an inviting toy for me and my friends. I knew now why Mother had consistently discouraged its extensive use as a toy. With enthusiastic help from Aunt Rubi and me, and using special nails and glue, Mother attached the skin to the skeleton as tautly as possible. My sister's gaval was reborn. Blessed by the absence of tattletales, it would live a happy and productive life. In fact, it outlived Father by many years. It is just possible that it is still alive today in a loving home that inherited it.

A year after Father died, when the mourning period had officially ended, my older brother, still living at home in his new role as the man of the house, bought Mother a shiny new, battery-operated, radio. The new master also weighed the pros and cons of electricity and, having ruled that it was not as dangerous as Father had feared, admitted it into our home. An electric fan and a large radio set followed. The gaval came out of the closet and contributed many enjoyable hours to the lives of the neighborhood youth who borrowed it from time to time.

Five or six years later, Mother herself took a pilgrimage to Mecca, at which time she gave the gaval to the teenage daughter of a friend. Not that she considered it a sin to play the instrument, she said. It was just that the neighbors would consider it below her dignity now. My brother and I teased her and pretended that we didn't believe her. "Of course you think it is a sin now," we contradicted her, "and you are sorry you ever played." "Don't be silly," she countered with the familiar, knowing smile on her lips, "if I considered playing the gaval sinful, would I give it to an innocent girl?" "No," I conceded, "you would have found a more innocent kid you could bribe to tear the gaval into pieces." Her smile disappeared for a moment when she replied: "No, no, I would have destroyed it myself."

MY FATHER'S WARDROBE

THE STREAM OF UNINTERRUPTED FOND MEMORIES of my father dries up essentially at the approximate age of seven, when I became aware of just how thoroughly "not with it" he was. (Were your folks, dear reader, with it when you were very young? If you are a parent, did your children often think you were not quite with it? I certainly wasn't with it, and my daughters knew it. Consider, for example, my not knowing the names of famous pop singers, and not even being ashamed of it! Now I compare myself to my father and shudder at the thought of how my daughters would have viewed him. Not at all with it? Totally without it?)

When I was seven, Father decided that the era of fun and frivolity had come to an end for me. Uncompromising discipline was to commence now, in order to prepare me for serious, austere adulthood. "*Agha*," as he was appropriately called by his offspring, meaning "master", was in his seventies at the time. But the way he dressed made him look centuries old to me. His traditional garments looked ridiculous, I thought to myself. All my friends' fathers whom I met wore more regular clothes and were of a more regular age. Some were rich and modern, some just rich, some poor but painfully conscious of fashions, and some just poor. But they all looked very young and they all wore clothes that didn't set them apart. Whenever my schoolmates told me that they had seen me with my "grandfather" in the park, I didn't correct them. Even the grandfathers I had seen with the kids looked younger and more with it than my father. God, I prayed, why couldn't I have one of those fathers who shaved their beards and wore a suit and tie? I would have forgiven him his age, even.

It is hard to understand it now, but Agha's appearance must have been an embarrassment to every member of my family who was alive when I was born. My mother accepted it as a matter of duty, like a good woman. But my oldest brother Kazem, a poet, a staunch follower of Frangi ways, and an aspiring teacher in modern schools, must have felt it more than the other family members. When he graduated from the Teachers' Training College in Tehran, and got his first pay check as a teacher, he observed the old tradition of spending it on substantial gifts for parents. His gift for Agha was a nicely tailored suit. Having a suit made normally required several fittings at the tailor's shop, but Kazem knew that Agha would have none of it. So, as I would later learn from my mother, he asked a friend of the family whose bodily proportions were close to those of Agha's, to pose as a mannequin for the tailor. Thus he was able to present the ready-made suit to Agha as a fait accompli.

That was the only modern garment Father ever owned and ever wore – infrequently, and reluctantly. Frugal Agha couldn't let the suit go to waste, but he made sure to wear it only on cold winter days, so he could conceal it under his nondescript, traditional overall, the *qabaa*, which made him look like images in my school books of twelfth-century scholars. (Which twelfth century, Western or Eastern, doesn't matter in this context. If I could tell from the images in my school books, all scholars who lived during the six hundred years between those two different twelfth centuries had used the services of the same immortal tailor.)

The suit had been made when I was a year old. When I was fourteen, it still played an occasional and semivisible part in Agha's winter dressing for the street. I found it a little odd that Kazem, aged around twenty-five at the time of presentation of the suit, still cared about reforming Agha, and still thought it possible. I, on the other hand, had accepted the impossibility by the age of puberty. Could it be that my brother had known a different, younger and less rigid, father many years before my time? It could also be that in those decades that preceded the period of all-out modernization, forced by the Shah of Iran, my father's apparel hadn't looked so out of place. There must have been at least some grandfathers around at that time, who dressed in ancient styles.

Frivolous! That is what my father thought of all forms of modern dress. Everything even slightly frivolous was acceptable to him only if you were a child, thereafter to be avoided at extreme costs. He was a reactionary but, luckily, not a militant one, so that "extreme" meant "as far as the law of the land could be interpreted to permit." Agha always wore a very simple qabaa, which changed only in thickness according to the season. The qabaa looked, with sufficient stretch of the imagination, like an out-of-style western overcoat, which was permitted by the Shah's Frangi dress codes. So he avoided trouble by never taking the overcoat off in the street even on hot summer days. After all, the government could hardly prosecute him for feeling cold in summer, or for dressing unfashionably.

The image of a qabaa, with the minute details of its shape and design, has remained engraved in my mind. Thirty years after Agha's death, after a gradual metamorphosis of my memories of him from hurtful to funny, I was able to redesign a qabaa from memory and tailor a very faithful copy. I wore it proudly to present myself as Omar Khayam at a Halloween costume party in Halifax, and it was a success. I felt that I could fit a twelfth-century scholar into full dress for any occasion.

The hat was another problem. Hatless men were allowed to be seen outdoors of course, but bare-headedness was too frivolous for Agha, almost a sin. So he wore the less offensive of the only two models of Western hats permitted by law: the cap with a visor, the "kepi", rather than the one with the rim all around it, the "chapeau". He also made me wear a hat outdoors whenever he could, that is, whenever I walked in the bazaar, where he or his friends could spot me. Fortunately, he let me wear my school uniform rather than insist on a miniature twelfth-century scholar's qabaa. He had no choice; school regulations insisted on this frivolity. In fairness to his memory, it should be said that he didn't have to send me to school at all, but he did. He had decided at some point that this was a necessary evil – for boys. For my sister, of course, it was too frivolous and too immodest to attend a modern school.

It is interesting where Agha drew his lines in accepting what he thought was absolutely minimal frivolity around him. One of his friends, whom I would learn to dislike intensely, had drawn his lines differently. When I was about fourteen, on one of his visits to our house, while sipping his obligatory tea which I had served, the guest decided to exchange pleasantries with the little boy. Did I go to school, he asked. Yes, I did. And what grade was I in? Proudly, I announced, "eighth", whereupon the man turned to my father with a dark red face. "Two grades too many", was his irrevocable verdict. "After elementary school, they teach only harmful stuff," he said. "And if they aren't teaching, they are playing games," he added. He admonished Agha to remedy the situation, hoping that it wasn't too late. Wasn't there some useful vocation that I could start learning, he asked, rather than frequenting these virtually godless schools?

What a disappointment! The man had fooled me: he wore a modern suit; he even had a chapeau on his head. He looked so regular, so with it. Up until now I would have easily traded my father for him. His frivolity lines, I had erroneously thought, were surely drawn with more liberal allowances than Agha's. Now I was scared. What if Agha took his advice seriously? What if Agha talked to other like-minded men, and decided enough was enough and I should stop all this modern education nonsense and learn something traditional? No, I consoled myself, if he wanted to do that, why had he allowed my older brothers to go through high school and even university? But again, he was older now and more exposed to open advice, given in conservative newspapers, which had been banned by the former Shah of Iran, but were proliferating after his forced abdication. They never tired of condemning the old regime for its sinful insistence on modernization.

Fortunately, Agha didn't listen to the guest. But the scary and confusing experience taught me to refine my criteria on his friends' degree of modernity. Had I observed the guest more carefully, I would have noted that he hadn't taken his chapeau off indoors; a good sign that he was not a truly westernized man. He didn't have a tie on and he wasn't clean shaven; two more signs of his adherence to strict versions of the Faith. On the other hand, he had chosen to seat himself in an armchair in our guest room, rather than insist, as the real traditionalists did, on sitting on the carpeted floor. This was a contrary sign. But, again, shouldn't I have noticed that he had left his shoes outside, unlike the ultra-modern guests, who, to the utter disgust of my mother, would enter any room with their shoes on? What about the way he drank his tea, cooling it off first by pouring it into a saucer? Why was I so blinded by his Frangi suit and hat?

The man had a point, I would come to the conclusion later. While it was true that Darwin didn't surface until the beginning of tenth grade, there was a lot of frivolity in school starting right with seventh grade: the Athletic Club, the Chess club, the Music club, the Year-book Club, the Theatre Club, the debating club, and so on. I joined the Modern Literature Club, but didn't tell any grownups – until they passed more than just my simple, now suspect, wardrobe test.

MY BEST FRIEND MAMADALI AND I, aged about eight and nine, were playing in his courtyard one summer afternoon when we were summoned by his grandmother, Saria, to help her save a life. The life belonged to the old woman who was the unequalled story-teller of the neighborhood, adored by all the kids. She had been bed-ridden for weeks, apparently for no reason that an affordable doctor could determine.

Saria took me and Mamadali to a far corner of her large garden. "Who is ready to pee?" she asked urgently. She needed the fluid from a young boy for medicinal purposes, she stated sternly when she noticed our bemusement. "Don't waste time," she said. Mamadali wasn't sure he was ready, so I complied by filling the tiny tea-glass Saria had brought along. There was no time for questions – not that she was in any mood to answer. She took the glass and rushed to the ailing neighbor's house, where my mother and a few other neighbor women were also visiting.

Mamadali and I resumed the little ball game that had been interrupted so rudely by his grandmother, but I couldn't help wondering what on earth Saria, a highly religious, meticulously observant person, would do with a glass-full of unclean urine. I knew that even a drop of it on her clothes would necessitate a ritual washing. If spilled on the carpet of the living room, it would entail a major purifying operation. If it penetrated the carpet and contaminated the floor, it would present a much graver problem: unless the floor could be exposed to direct sunlight, there was virtually no way to cleanse it, except for breaking up the floor and removing as large a chunk of it as necessary to ensure that the resulting hole in the floor was free from contamination. What possible medicinal value could such a disgusting substance have? Was it for external or, God forbid, internal use? Wasn't there a strict prohibition by the highest authorities of the Faith on the consumption of all things impure? I knew that, besides being fanatically attentive to religious matters, Saria was also a strong believer in folk medicine and the occult. Purported influences on our lives of celestial bodies, beneficial properties of rain water collected on certain days of the year, and the strong advisability of not clipping finger nails on Wednesdays and Saturdays did not escape her attention. Nevertheless, it was difficult to understand her seeming ability to compromise on points of faith.

This must have been a real emergency, I thought to myself as I left Mamadali's house, hoping that my mother would shed some light on the matter when she came home, but I would have to wait a couple of hours for that. I knew that our baby-sitter couldn't be of any help whatsoever. Neither I nor Mamadali could hope for much enlightenment from his grandmother. Saria was just too serious an adult to waste valuable time with kids. In fact, Mamadali was always uncomfortable around her, and sometimes scared to death. He had suffered quite a few inordinately harsh rounds of punishment at Saria's hands for what everybody else thought were minor childish infractions. Whenever Mamadali disobeyed her, she would threaten to fill his mouth with hot pepper. I was once an eyewitness to this disciplinary action which caused Mamadali, perhaps a mere six-year-old kid at the time, to scream incessantly for a good part of an hour. I could hear him from my house, which was adjacent to his, and to which I had fled in horror. When I returned after the screams had subsided, Saria was feeding Mamadali spoonfuls of sweet pudding and explaining to him that the punishment was for his own good and he would only understand when he had kids of his own some day.

When Mamadali was just over two years old, Saria had made Mamadali's father, her very young son, divorce Mamadali's mother, thereafter assuming the roles of mother and father. The dutiful son, only fifteen at the time of his marriage arranged by Saria and the bride's parents, had had absolutely no say in these transactions. Nor, of course, had the bride who was even younger than the groom. "The bride wasn't obedient enough," Saria would reply curtly to anyone who dared to enquire about the divorce. Even mentioning the name of Mamadali's mother in his presence was strictly forbidden by Saria. I had a hard time following this rule; I still had fond memories of the young, energetic, funloving girl-bride who never failed to keep Mamadali and me entertained whenever she took a break from her daily household chores.

Mamadali dreaded the biannual sessions of bloodletting ordered by Saria. This service, considered by her to be indisputably essential for the maintenance of a child's health, was performed by certain ex-nomadic practitioners who lived in an outlying district of Tabriz. (Their traditional Gypsy ways, deemed uncivilized and unsafe by the former king, Reza Shah, had come to an end a dozen years earlier, when they were ordered to stop roaming around the country once and for all.) They now administered legal therapeutic massages and prescribed semilegal medicines. They also performed illegal operations, for which they preferred to make house calls. Every spring and fall, Saria subjected the willing adults among her relatives and acquaintances together with the unwilling Mamadali to the operation, which consisted in making several vertical cuts of about six centimeters in length on the back of the patient's upper body and collecting what seemed to me about a bottle of blood, even from tiny Mamadali. But my memory must be exaggerating a bit here. It was enough, however, to give Mamadali a temporary, postoperative, pale complexion. But what was this small discomfort compared to insurance against that long list of ailments Saria cited for my mother's benefit, offering her and me the privilege of inclusion in the seasonal immunization at discount group rates? Mother had to reiterate and reconfirm her emphatic "no" every season. This provided Saria with a good reason to admonish her whenever a flu hit me but spared Mamadali – with a sincere "I warned you."

No kid in the neighborhood liked Saria. Quite a few of us called Saria's gentle, kindly older sister "Great Auntie," but none of us entertained the idea of calling Saria anything but "Saria Khanum." The added word was a formal title of respect attached to the name of any grown-up woman, simply meaning "lady." All of us kids feared Saria, but not nearly as fiercely as Mamadali did. We just tried to avoid her as much as possible.

Mamadali's large courtyard had a sizeable garden, replete with grape vines on one side, and an open area, suitable for many of the games we liked to play, on the other. Great Auntie let us play there and even supplied us with refreshments. All we had to do was leave Mamadali's courtyard before Saria came home. Great Auntie called her Saria, but she was the only one who didn't attach "Khanum" to the name. (I find it slightly uncomfortable even now, after more than a half century, to refer to her by her mere given name. But I will resist the weird feeling and stick to the short, undecorated form.)

Fortunately for the kids, Saria was very seldom home. On the rare occasion when the kids forgot her arrival time, or she came home early, she would immediately find an excuse to make the kids leave. "Didn't I tell you," she would yell at Mamadali, "not to treat this house as a public stable?" We would start gathering our toys in a hurry to leave. "Who is going to clean all this mess when they leave?" she would ask, gradually raising the decibel levels. She treated me more tolerantly, mainly because of her overwhelming respect for my old and wise father who could answer all her religious questions. (I often thought that Saria would make a more suitable wife for my father than my mother did: he was also a disciplinarian, though not as cruel as Saria; also a serious follower of the Faith, though not as ascetic as her.) It was okay if Saria came home and found only me playing with Mamadali.

Unlike any other woman in the neighborhood, Saria never did any housework. She left it all to her older sister, Great Auntie. I suppose she justified this by the fact that her son, Mamadali's father, had been the sole bread-winner of the household ever since Great Auntie, a childless widow, moved in with them. Saria's own husband and her only other child had died tragically, leaving her in a perpetual state of mourning. Apparently, it was as a result of this tragedy that Saria's religiosity escalated to such heights as to earn her the nickname "Pious." This name was consistently used, by the other neighborhood women, themselves quite religious but only by normal standards, mainly to distinguish her from another, "more normal," Saria living on the block.

Oblivious to how she was seen by others, Saria absented herself from home almost every weekday, except for a brief lunch and siesta break. On summer weekends, she purposefully attended to her vineyard, enclosing the clusters of grapes, as soon as they started to ripen, in the numerous individual little bags of cloth she had sewed during winter weekends. This was to protect the harvest from birds, but was ineffective against stealthy attacks by Mamadali and me. There were usually so many bagfuls of delicious grapes, invitingly hanging on the vines, that a couple of missing bagfuls per day would certainly go unnoticed by Saria.

"I know what you are doing," Great Auntie once said when she caught the two of us trying to get rid of the evidence after a guilty feast on the sweet contents of several large bags right off the vines. "Don't throw away those bags;" she pleaded, "I'll wash them and place them back on Saria's pile of spare bags. There are so many of them, she'll never notice." We were actually too scared to throw the empty bags in the waste basket, certain that Saria would find them if we did. We had already invented and repeatedly applied what we thought was a permanent solution to the problem: we would put a small stone in each empty bag, tie it up with its own attached lace and project it carefully so that it would land on the flat roof of the house without breaking windows. We were now glad to enlist the unexpected help of such a kindly accomplice as Great Auntie, and forgo our own method of disposal with the potentially hazardous trajectory. The accumulated colorful, though partially deteriorated, bags with a stone in each, would raise eyebrows several years later, when the mud-and-straw roof was due for a recoating. Fortunately, the eyebrows wouldn't be Saria's, but only Mamadali's father's. On that occasion we would easily tell him our secret. "Let us confess to your grandmother too," I would say. "Are you kidding?" Mamadali would reply, not totally in jest, "I don't have half the tolerance for hot pepper that I had when I was five or six."

On weekdays, Saria's mornings and afternoons were devoted to attending at least two "circuits." "Circuit" was the name by which the rotating social gatherings of the zealously faithful were known. There were separate circuits going, for men and women, throughout the year. Once in a while, it would be Saria's turn to entertain the women in one of her circuits. The meetings were substantial affairs, formally presided over by an amateur preacher-singer. Saria often managed to find a woman for the job (not a trivial accomplishment in itself). The female leader of the meeting would recite passages from passion plays, in a soft voice – in order to protect the men within possible earshot from the sinful enjoyment of female voice. These quiet lamentations on the selfless lives and deaths of the patron saints of the Faith never failed to produce the expected result: collective, loud crying and wailing that sounded utterly uncontrollable. Yet the wailing came to an abrupt end when the singing stopped for a lengthy intermission, and freshly brewed tea was served with sugar and lemon, accompanied with chunks of grape-syrup halvah. ("How is it," a reader may wonder, "that the cries and wails of the female crowd were allowed to subject innocent male eavesdroppers to the multiple auditory sin?" Such a reader would be relieved to learn that, unlike the solo female voice, a chorus of women was decreed by the custodians of the Faith to have no sin-producing effect on the male ear.)

Over the sweet-and-sour tea, the atmosphere was decidedly social, and the conversation in the circuit would turn to exchange of recipes, for both food and folk medicine, reports of attempts at matchmaking, and news of upcoming circuit meetings. The participants, predominantly over the age of fifty, peppered every report with references to the Almighty or the Prophets and Saints. "Did you hear about the young Mash Karim's sudden death, may God forgive him, from a heart attack?" I once heard a member of the circuit ask. "What did you expect?" another conjectured to the unanimously approving nods of those who were listening, "I hear he was a closet drinker, may the burden of libel rest on the shoulders of my sources if they were not telling the truth, God forbid." A third member had more information: "I don't know about his drinking, but my husband saw him once in the Armenian quarters, near a pub after midnight, and do you know what he was doing? He was urinating against a wall, standing – like an unclean dog, disregarding the Sacred Tradition; no wonder he was having trouble with his bladder in the last years of his life." Yet another member sought to clarify the matter further: "And that modern, young Frangi doctor didn't help either. He may be a schooled doctor, as they call them these days, but does he know a fraction of what my unschooled but old, experienced doctor, may God lend him a long life, knows? No. Why the young doctor himself is not above drinking, I hear. While he was studying in Paris, he learned all the bad habits and customs of the French, may God direct them all to the Right Path. His fashionable necktie and Chapeau won't fool me, I tell you."

Saria, to be fair to her memory, did not condone the gossipy turn the conversation sometimes took during these intermissions, and reminded the transgressors of the sin they were in the process of committing. "We should repent, and speak no more about Mash Karim;" she said on this occasion, "who knows, maybe he was forgiven. Don't forget that if he shed just one sincere tear in the mourning of our beloved Martyred Saints, with total faith in their mediating powers before the Almighty, then God has to keep His promise and protect him from the fires of Hell. Yes, even those who have succumbed to the Satan in the bottle." The audience, duly awakened, sipped the last cups of sweet-and-sour tea in a reflective mood, consumed some halvah, and prepared for more sincere outpouring of cries of grief at another round of the requiem following the intermission.

The circuit session over, the good women covered themselves from head to toe before venturing into the street. They did not expose their faces and hands like their more modern, but quite religious neighbors. To be on the safe side, they went just a bit further than the Scripture had prescribed for pious women. My mother, though deeply religious, was modern enough to keep her eyes uncovered, to have doubts about most of Saria's outrageous medical advice, and to think that the whole idea of circuits was overdoing it a bit unless it was restricted to the mourning months of the lunar year in which the martyrdom of the Saints had actually occurred.

"What was the pee for?" I asked Mother when she finally came home from her long visit to the sick neighbor. "Saria Khanum fed it to the patient, of course," Mother informed me. "Did the patient know what she was drinking?" I wondered aloud, curious and disgusted. "No," Mother said, "that was the whole point; the patient wasn't supposed to know until she drank it all." It turned out that Saria had meant to "stun" the sick woman after she had imbibed a generous portion of the liquid remedy mixed with sweet tea, and thus "snap the demon out of her." I was becoming more curious by the minute. "But, isn't it forbidden to eat or drink impure things?" I asked. " 'This was a desperate case, requiring desperate measures,'" Mother quoted Saria as saying. "How did Saria Khanum decide that the patient had a demon hiding in her?" I wanted to know. Mother reminded me of the time Saria gave me one of her usual tests to determine the cause of the ache I felt in my legs. On that occasion, she had decided already, I don't remember how, that my ailment was a "scare pain." So she proceeded to find out what or who had scared me into this pain. I have a vivid memory of the procedure and its miraculous outcome.

To find the source of the scare, Saria melted a small amount of bees-wax with minute doses of other ingredients. She had me lying on my back, with a flat bowl of cold water resting on my chest. She then poured the hot, melted bees-wax in the bowl. Instantaneously, Saria and I recognized the culprit as the neighborhood stray dog into whose facsimile the large wax drop had transformed itself. I had in fact been scared of the dog. Saria, like any other pious person, detested the presence of the unclean beast in the vicinity, where uneducated kids might inadvertently touch it and forget to go through the ritual washing afterwards. Yet she fed the dog daily, in obedience of the dictum of the Faith that required being kind to forsaken children and animals. I imagined quietly and with amusement that if Mamadali was ever given this test, the bees-wax would immediately turn into a full statuette of Saria Khanum herself.

The source of the scare pain having been easily detected, Saria suggested several possible remedies, to the least invasive of which Mother consented. Thus Saria produced, from a small case in an upper drawer of a chest in her living room, a very large ring, made of white cotton, on which appropriate prayers had been inscribed in permanent black ink. She then instructed me to pass through the ring seven times. I did. Then Saria kissed the cotton ring, pronounced me cured, and deferentially returned the device to its protective case for future use. I was hugely impressed by the diagnostic powers of bees-wax. Ten years later, in college, the memory of the incident would provide me with much needed ammunition to annoy a psychology professor whom my classmates and I particularly disliked: As the professor went on and on, singing the praise of Rorschach and his "useful, innovative ink-blot test," I would raise my hand and beg to differ. "How could it be called innovative," I would ask, "if an old, functionally illiterate woman to whose gypsy mentors all advances in science had ceased centuries ago, could have a perfect, three-dimensional version of Rorschach's flat trick up her sleeve?" Then to the chagrin of the professor and to the delight of my fellow-students, I would proceed to give a short account of Saria's wax test.

The matter of medicinal pee continued to puzzle me for weeks after it was administered to our beloved story-teller. All of us kids were happy by the recovery of the patient, toward which, according to my older brother, my contribution had played no part at all. An impertinent woman, apparently as puzzled as I was about the impure prescription, dared to pose the question directly in Saria's presence. Saria started to enlighten her gently, by reminding her of the occasion when another bed-ridden neighbor was ordered by her doctor to take brandy. "And which is more impure? Brandy or pee?" Saria asked. "Of course brandy," the questioner conceded. "Yes," Saria confirmed, "yes, given brandy's evil character; may the homes of the faithful never see its color within their walls." Saria then explained that a pious and reliable doctor was allowed by the Fathers of the Faith to prescribe whatever was necessary; even if it was the most evil matter imaginable, unless there was a benign alternative, needless to say. "And who is more pious?" she demanded to know, "Me or that expensive doctor, schooled in Paris, who shaves his beard close, wears a *Frangi* hat, and won't even give up his red tie in mourning months, whose son plays with a pet dog just as infidels' children do, and whose wife never covers her hair in public?" There was no question that Saria was the more pious of the two.

The seeker of truth, apparently not quite satisfied with Saria's explanations, made one last attempt at clarification. "A pious and reliable doctor," she said meekly, repeating Saria's own words. Her emphasis on the word "doctor," tentative though it was, changed the tone of the conversation. Saria, now radiating indignation, was determined to set the woman straight. "Who is more reliable?" she asked rhetorically, "Who cured your own son who was wetting his bed at the age of ten? And are you forgetting that your doctor couldn't do a thing about it?" The intimidated woman felt it necessary to interrupt Saria and gratefully acknowledge that her son had indeed been cured after eating barbecued sheep testicles, a remedy prescribed by Saria. "There," said Saria with as sisterly a smile as she could manage, and proceeded to neutralize the potential antagonist for good: "How many patients have died, so far, under your good doctor's care? How many more will he kill before he grows older and more experienced?" After a pause, presumably to allow the subdued questioner some mental counting time, came the short, but definitive, proof of Saria's superiority to the young doctor as a healer: "Tell me, as God is our witness. Have my remedies ever killed anyone?"

"TAKE THE BASKET AND COME ALONG," said my father, "we have shopping to do for the party tonight." My mother had been working hard for a whole week, with a neighborly woman's help, in preparation for this evening's big dinner. This was one of each summer's two or three dinners to which Father's friends and business acquaintances were invited – about fifteen or twenty of them.

Mother had a reputation for being an excellent cook, given the right ingredients. The right ingredients were not always available in Tabriz, except in summertime. Mother immensely enjoyed the preparations with the best and freshest herbs and vegetables for these occasions, which provided exemption from the usual everyday considerations of tight economy. She simply told Father what was needed for the feast and Father bought it and I carried it home. I didn't mind contributing my labor at all, in anticipation of tasty and plentiful leftovers for several days after the big dinner. (During the dinner time, both Mother and I would be too busy with hospitality chores to enjoy what we had a chance to gulp down.)

I took the basket and started out with Father toward the bazaar. I expected this last shopping trip before the big dinner to be very short. We had, during the preceding five or six mornings, gradually provided Mother with the ingredients she needed for each day's planned partial preparations. Just the day before, we had bought fresh vegetables. There was only one thing left for this last day, and now we were going to get it: the mutton. Meat had to be bought on the last day, since we had no refrigeration facilities in the house.

The mutton shops in my neighborhood always had just enough fresh meat to last for the day. In summertime, nobody would buy mutton that had left the slaughter house more than a few hours earlier. This was a particularly hot summer morning. Also, Father and I had been delayed at home by Mother's last-minute calculations on how much meat to buy, so Father's favorite mutton shop was already sold out. We kept walking. The second and third shops didn't have nearly enough meat. We got more and more discouraged as we passed by the mutton shops with dwindling supplies. Even the total supply of all the shops we encountered wasn't enough. We were now getting desperate. Father started to contemplate the unthinkable: he considered buying beef instead.

We had bought beef before, but only for our own consumption and to save money. Mutton in Tabriz, or in villages around it, was three times as expensive as beef, a ratio well justified by quality. It was widely believed that only working cows were slaughtered at retirement for the beef market. Self-respecting hosts never served beef to a guest whose discretion they couldn't fully count on. My grandmother never allowed herself to forget the shameful occasion on which a family friend, who had lived in Russia for many years, invited her to dinner and served her borscht made with beef. "How low-class can you get?" she kept wondering for months afterwards, "and you know how rich this family is too! Why even their maid seemed embarrassed serving us the beefy soup."

When Father started toward the beef shop, I made an attempt to warn him. "Mother would die," I said, "if she had to serve beef to our guests." He said that there was no choice and allowed himself a few moments' reflection on whether or not to continue this serious discussion with a mere kid. Then he reminded me of the one earlier, very exceptional, occasion on which Mother had, after considerable toil, succeeded in making a small amount of beef tolerable for the consumption of close family guests. I knew that even if it were possible for Mother to pull it off at this late hour, Father would tell the guests what kind of meat they were devouring. The embarrassment of a single guest finding out was for him much more humiliating than the simple admission of the necessary transgression. So I tried to persuade him to walk on and look further for proper meat.

We came across an old acquaintance of Father's, who knew of a mutton shop in his neighborhood that apparently had facilities to keep the meat fresh for more than a few hours. I was happy to hear this. So was Father, despite misgivings about "unnatural and forced" ways in which "the life of dead meat was prolonged." Although kerosene-operated refrigerators were now available, to alleviate his inordinate fear of electricity in homes, he would under no circumstances trust such complicated and unfamiliar gadgets in his house. It took us another fifteen or twenty minutes to walk to the fancy mutton shop in the modern part of the city, where we seldom shopped. "They are bound to ask for their fathers' blood money," Father muttered on the way, referring to the expected high prices in this neighborhood, "but we'll just have to pay for their expensive equipment and their decorations as well as their mutton."

Sure enough, the shop was well stocked, but not in the same manner as those we were used to. In our shops in the traditional Tabriz bazaar, large, full bodies of mutton were hung from ceiling hooks, and customers chose what part of which body they wanted. This was very important for Father. He had his own criteria for suitability of various meats for consumption, including the natural color of the various parts of the meat, their relative sizes, and so on.

The most important criterion was the gender of the animal: it just had to be male. "The Modicum" said so. This was the affectionate way in which Father referred to a book that he consulted on all "scientific matters." Its long and very informative title, as explained in the introduction, could be translated roughly as "A Modicum of Everything Needed by Everybody in Everyday Living." It had verses by which to memorize the names, in Persian and Arabic, of solar months, lunar months, and Chinese years. It gave names of the planets in several languages. It identified important countries, main bodies of water, and historic figures. The Modicum also showed how to convert measurements, to decide on locations of residence and business, to determine lucky hours and days of the month for weddings, circumcisions, and long trips. A substantial chapter was dedicated to choosing the right food and right medicine with the right dosage for each age group and for each season.

In the section entitled "On the Nature of Various Classes of Foods and their relevance to the Health of Human Body," the Modicum classified all meat from female mammals "as extremely cold in nature." When so designated, a food item was only good for kids, adolescents, and people suffering from certain rare ailments. Otherwise, it was considered to be a health hazard whose gravity increased dramatically with advancing age. Father and most of his guests belonged to the category that faced the greatest risk unless they avoided cold-natured food items at all cost. Father, a septuagenarian himself at the time, stuck as faithfully as possible to the recommended warm-natured meals, supplemented every morning with some hot-natured items, just to be on the safe side. The supplements included walnuts, dates, honey, and ginger. These were, of course, forbidden to all kids my age. If Mother let me have a walnut or a couple of dates now and then, it was always with the understanding that Father was not to know. "Why couldn't a kid eat figs instead of dates?" he would demand to know. He, of course, wouldn't touch a fig or a watermelon, such notoriously cold-natured items according to the Modicum.

In the mutton shops we frequented, it was easy for Father to satisfy his essential requirement: he simply chose cuts from a piece that still had the male organ attached to it. Apparently, the butchers had many old customers who owned copies of the Modicum, because they tried very hard to keep the organs attached to the hung bodies of mutton until the last cut was sold. I have vivid memories of one particular shop that happened to be on my way to grade school. The mutton pieces hung from the ceiling hooks of this shop always had the same uniform length, but they varied in girth. The bodies all started with approximately identical dimensions in the early morning when they arrived fresh from the city slaughter-house. But with the obvious goal of keeping suspicious customers happy, the butcher kept cutting around their essential organs, making them thinner and thinner in the process. By noontime every weekday, upon passing by the shop again on the way home from school, I witnessed a spectacular display of half a dozen thread-thin, almost five-foot-long, bodies of mutton with only one proud protrusion in the middle.

Informed of Father's requirement, the keeper of the fancy mutton shop presented a few spotless and very fresh-looking shoulders and legs of mutton. Seeing how uncomfortable Father looked, and knowing why, he swore that he had just personally cut the pieces from a ram. He even headed to the rear of the shop in an attempt to prove his claim by retrieving the missing and discarded organ from a bowl of treats reserved for his cat. I prayed silently but as urgently as I could for Father to trust the man. Father hesitated for only a few seconds, during which he decided not to place the health of his guests at risk. He told me to take the empty basket and accompany him back to the bazaar and the beef butcher. "Sorry," he said to the visibly irate shopkeeper, "but I require proof, and the proof must be attached."

"YOU WILL SHARE YOUR SANDWICH WITH ME TODAY," said the new boy in our school sternly, addressing one of my classmates whose box lunch had attracted his attention. After a brief reflection on the size of the new kid, the classmate decided to obey. The large and chubby boy, who would soon establish himself as the prime bully of the class, was starting third grade at the unconventional time of late winter. His family had just moved to Tabriz and taken residence in my neighborhood. None of the neighbors knew anything about the newcomers yet, except that the head of the family was a foreman in the new leather processing factory.

"*Pota*," as every student would soon start calling the boy behind his back, literally meaning "chubby," couldn't have arrived at a more opportune time for extortion. The spring festivities surrounding *Nowruz*, the Iranian new year, were coming soon, and all of us kids would have lots of goodies available for "sharing" with Pota. He seemed to be particularly fond of colored eggs and hard candy, which every kid counted on getting a good supply of. He started to place Nowruz orders right away, consistently using the future tense – a habit evidently acquired from his father ordering the leather-workers around. "You will bring me half of your colored eggs," he said to me. I did comply. I delivered to him about half a dozen of my accumulated eggs following Nowruz, wondering how he could trust me with the count.

For the kids of my age in my neighborhood of Tabriz, Nowruz spelled the best season of the entire year, even better than the long summer vacation. No school for the first fourteen days of spring. No homework. A new suit and new shoes to be seen in. Colored eggs, chocolate, and coins from friends of the family and even from remote relatives who visited only once a year. More treats when we paid them a return visit.

The traditional, and mandatory, annual visits to friends and relatives started with Nowruz and continued for almost two weeks. One had to be prepared for the unannounced arrival of visitors day and night. This meant, among other things, that a fair supply of pastries, cookies, candies, and fresh fruit had to be maintained at home. My parents, like most other parents I knew, subscribed to the motto, "the best for the guest." Mother was a true fanatic on this matter. Nothing that we could possibly afford was too good for guests. Besides, what would they, the distant relatives who set eyes on the inside of our home but once a year, think if it looked as though we couldn't afford good cookies and candy to go with their tea?

We had two rooms prepared for the occasion, one for men and one for women. Unrelated people couldn't be entertained in mixed company. Not in my neighborhood anyway – except for the one Westernized family labeled by everyone else as "*Frangi-maab*", a term uttered with scorn by some and with envy by others. Each room had several tables decked out with goodies to edify visitors. There was a supply of cigarettes on each table. There were also a few long pipes and hobble-bubbles, with bags of tobacco beside them on a corner table in each room. Father smoked only cigarettes and Mother didn't smoke at all, but many of their guests did, and a good host always provided the opportunity for guests to indulge in their preferred pleasures.

We knew few people who owned phones. Besides, warning a host of an intended visit wasn't considered a good idea, especially by the unwired majority. It implied self-importance on the caller's part. It also deprived the host of the customary protestation that the offerings weren't nearly worthy of such a dear guest: proper preparations would have been made if only the host knew of the impending honor of visitation in advance.

Hosts, too, had their visiting duties to attend to. Yet it was bad form not to be home when a guest arrived. This obvious anomaly was dealt with in various ways. A logical system had existed before my time, at least in Tabriz, and Father never tired of lamenting its demise and cursing the advent of modern times for causing the current unsatisfactory state of affairs. The old way had been very simple: the first day of festivities, Nowruz proper, was reserved for calling on family elders and other people of status; each succeeding day was then designated as visiting day for the dwellers of one of the well-defined districts of the city. "If we still had the system," said Father, "we would only have to be home on the first and sixth days." The first day, because Father was in his mid seventies and hence a qualified elder of the extended family;

and the sixth day, because it would have been our district's designated day.

Father had no tolerance for the modern solutions to this hospitality problem. He immensely disliked, for example, the practice of some of his Frangi associates who placed an ad in the local newspaper, regretfully informing the public of their inability to perform their important duties, due to travel. "I bet they are not even traveling," he said, "they are just hiding in their houses, those mean spirits. Besides, what makes travel so necessary now?" Travel for pleasure was certainly not a necessity in my household. We traveled only if we absolutely had too. Thus Father had stopped all travel after his last business trips to Russia and Turkey decades before. Mother had never left Tabriz since her arrival there from her home town of Salmas, in her early teens. During the last year of World War One, it had become absolutely necessary for her family to travel. This was to minimize the number of male members of the family subject to murder in the Salmas Massacre. My sister had left Tabriz at the age of twenty five, when her husband's business necessitated the move. Neither of my two older brothers had left home until they were eighteen, at which age it became necessary for them to travel to Tehran and start college. In eight years' time, I calculated expectantly, it would also be necessary for me to travel.

Other Frangi-maab citizens of Tabriz announced, again in the newspapers, that "in order not to miss the pleasure of the company of beloved friends and honored associates," they planned to be home on a fixed day "from 10 to 21 hours." "What a good solution," said Mother, "they save a lot of money and headache, yet they are able to pull their resources together for one day of hospitality they can be proud of." Father was not so impressed. "Who do they think they are, kings and queens? Besides, this is not a logical solution at all. Just imagine everybody doing it. We'd go crazy running from one distant neighborhood to another every day for several days, from 10 to 21 hours." He pronounced "twenty one" with a mock flourish of hand and toss of head. Using the twenty-four-hour clock for telling time was to him an affectation akin to speaking with a cultivated French accent.

In my household we resorted to the more common method of dealing with the problem: at least one of us three stayed home for the duration. My duties doubled whenever Father and Mother were both out on their respective manly and womanly visits. I answered the door, and with as much grace as I could muster, led the unannounced visitors to one of the two segregated guest rooms as if my parents were home. I was still in my "immature age," not yet forbidden the unhindered company of women. I took the guests' coats, hats, and umbrellas, and when asked again about my parents, I replied that they would be coming home soon. The socially correct lying was far from original, and the guests expected it. They even complimented me on how well I had performed. A female guest would say, "Well, well, what a nice, gracious little host; I would consider you as a good suitor for my daughter when you grow up." The compliment wasn't original either.

The samovar kept humming in the kitchen, ready for making hot fresh tea in short notice. Each room was kept comfortably warm by a fireplace. I ran back and forth between the kitchen and the guest rooms, and between men's and women's quarters when necessary, offering refreshments. I attended to my hosting duties happily, in anticipation of my self-negotiated compensation. Each time my charges left, and before Mother or Father came home, I rewarded myself with a generous amount of cakes and cookies. If they found out, they would both worry too much; Father about my getting sick, and Mother about the next guests not having enough to eat. Need I say that I considered my approved ration of goodies at the end of each day highly inadequate?

Just before Nowruz, during the fourth-grade year, my sister in Tehran sent us a most welcome gift of imported halvah by mail. This was no ordinary halvah. I had heard about it from friends, but not yet seen it. It was, I would later learn, made mainly of honey, sesame, and a "secret ingredient." I had tasted, but not liked, a cheap local imitation. There was another variety of traditional, home-made, halvah that I enjoyed frequently. Far more familiar to the middle and poorer classes than the exotic concoction at hand, this variety required a great deal of labor, but no honey or sesame (both expensive commodities) and no secret ingredient. The gift halvah arrived in the form of a large rectangular cube, much like a huge chunk of cheese and I looked forward to unwrapping and tasting it.

Fifty five years later, the New-York-Times reviewer of Elaine Sciolino's travel book, "Persian Mirrors," would wonder about the meaning of the Persian proverb, "Have patience, and your unripe grapes will turn to halvah."

Given only the fancy recipe for halvah, the saying would, understandably, sound strange to the Western ear. The responsibility would lie wholly with Sciolino's local experts in Iran, no doubt citizens more prosperous than most, who were capable of thoroughly missing the point. The main ingredient of poor man's halvah is grape syrup. Thus if you have enough patience, the unripe grapes will ripen in time; then the grapes will be made into the required thick syrup, which also takes substantial time and labor; and finally, the syrup will be used together with flour, oil, and turmeric (or a minute amount of saffron if affordable) to make halvah – finally to reward your patience.

We unwrapped the gift from my sister, and Mother cut a small piece for each member of the family to taste. Heavenly stuff. Unfortunately, Father decided that the delicacy was "too hot in nature" according to his authoritative book in traditional medicine, and therefore unsuitable for consumption by children in large quantities. Large quantities meant anything more than the equivalent of a teaspoonful a day. Mother didn't believe in Father's fanatical adherence to his book, and would secretly increase my daily ration a bit. But, unfortunately again, she believed firmly in the priority of guests. This halvah was definitely guest material.

Mother shaped the halvah into small, hexagonal pieces, each intended for a single serving to a guest. She neatly arranged the pieces on plates to be proudly displayed on the two guest rooms' tables. Hoping that my guests would spare the hexagons, I made a point of starting my dutiful offerings to guests with the other goodies off the corner tables. I would carry each plate around the room, as dictated by custom, and stop before each guest, who either took something or politely declined. I would then wait for some minutes before starting a new round with another plate or tray. This was all done correctly according to etiquette. All I had to do was to pass the halvah round last, and pray that Mother and Father would take their time returning home.

Either the guests had also fallen in love with the delicious hexagons, or they were playing a sadistic game with the little me, because an inordinate number of them discreetly refused to take anything else. "I'll teach you polite gluttons a lesson," I thought to myself, and extended the time intervals between servings. Self-respecting ladies and gentleman would never think of getting up and walking to the corner table to help themselves. So I enjoyed watching a few of my charges who, seemingly determined not to leave before tasting the exotic morsels, lingered on and made more small talk. My resolve weakened only once. That was when a guest, no longer able to contain himself, spoke of his curiosity about the hexagons, a treat hitherto unknown to him. There was no way out, and I had to expedite the halvah round.

As the end of the visiting period for the new year approached, I became aware of the real possibility that on the thirteenth day of Nowruz few hexagons would be left for me to enjoy without guilt. I knew that, according to an unwritten pact of conspiracy between Mother and me, which protected me from the excesses of Father's food-and-health dogma, I would have most of the leftover halvah to myself after the twelfth day of Nowruz. I had gotten accustomed by now to guiltless conspiracy in these matters. I kept fighting the dread of a total loss. I amused myself by imagining I had placed an announcement in every newspaper in Tabriz, warning the public about the possible health hazards of "secret ingredients in certain imported sweets."

In the last days of Nowruz I felt the necessity for desperate measures. Using the opportunity of a slow period between visitors, with Father and Mother both out, I took a sharp knife from the kitchen and performed a delicate, collective, surgical operation on the remaining hexagons. Painstakingly, I cut a very thin sliver off each side of every single one of them, reducing the size of each hexagon ever so slightly and undetectably, without altering its shape. I enjoyed the bounty and still ended up with the same number of hexagons as before. The new pieces were, I would later learn in school, geometrically "similar" to the original ones with a "similarity ratio" very close to one. I had time to marvel at the results of my successful experiment before the next guest arrived, but I knew that the results could not be reproduced indefinitely.

During the second careful operation the next day, I exercised a great deal of self-control in deciding the dimensions of the severed slivers. Still, when Mother came home and entered the women's guest room, she moved the halvah tray to another corner. "The heat from the fireplace is reducing those morsels," she complained. I thanked God that the halvah tray in the men's guest room had also been placed near the fireplace. I decided to put an end to the halvah surgery.

A very happy ending to the halvah saga came from an unlikely source in the form of a belated visit to Mother by Pota's mother, accompanied by Pota himself. Their family, having lived in the neighborhood for a year now, were still considered new arrivals. They had not yet passed their tests to qualify as full-fledged neighbors in this predominantly conservative district. For one thing, the man of the family was suspected of being a beer-drinker on weekends. For another, the family spoke with an implacable accent. But the boy was a friend of sorts to me by now. During the preceding year, Pota had either mellowed or reformed. Maybe my helping him with his arithmetic problems in school played a part in this gradual transformation. On this visit, we started to chat about the Nowruz gifts we had gathered. "I got a whole box of that stuff from my father's company head," he said to my great surprise and envy, and pointed to the hexagonal objects of my desire. I said I loved them. "How many colored eggs have you got?" he asked. "Fewer than twenty," I said cautiously. Pota was delighted by the answer, and made me an offer I couldn't refuse: fifteen eggs for his small box of imported halvah.

INK FOR LIFE

NURSING A COLD AT HOME ON A WINTER DAY, Father was la-
zily leafing through the pages of "the Modicum," the book
that he had owned and valued for more than sixty years as
his unique and indisputable authority on almost everything
other than religious matters. His random perusal stopped
when he came across a tempting recipe for making black ink.

Between his business correspondence and my elementary school work, the two of us went through a fair amount
of ink each year. I also used a lot of ink practicing Persian
calligraphy. This was the only art form Father whole-heartedly approved of. In fact, he saw it as an essential part of a
boy's education, a pedagogical vision which led to compulsory, extremely disciplined, and very long daily drills for me.
He had detected my "natural talent" for this noblest of arts,
and was determined not to let it go to waste. After first grade,
my school permitted no pencil as a writing instrument, and
certainly no fountain pen. Blue ink was allowed, but black
was the preferred color. Father didn't allow anything but
black. Thus more and more black ink would be needed as I
progressed to higher grades in school.

A combination of frugality and curiosity induced Father to try the ink recipe given in the Modicum. It was very simple; all it required was soot, water, and something called "Arabian gum." Upon my arrival from school that day, he ordered me to go to the drugstore and get a packet of this ingredient. The dark-purple substance, hardened gum from an uncommon plant and used mostly for medicinal purposes, had to be ground. This was hard work, but Father and I accomplished it in half a day. Now the soot that the recipe required had to be "very fine and soft," so Father decided that the variety easily obtainable from the fireplace wouldn't do, a decision that my mother and I would come to regret.

It seemed that many bottles of ink, possibly enough to last a lifetime, could be had for pennies. Father proudly announced that he knew how to make the soft fine soot the recipe called for. We would light a small kerosene lamp, one of the many we owned and used around the unelectrified house, and pull the wick up slightly, so that the burning would be incomplete. Two wooden stands of appropriate height would then be found or fashioned by Father to hold a plate about an inch above the top of the lamp. The required extra-soft, ink-worthy soot would gather on the plate. I thought the idea was very ingenious. Mother said nothing, but frowned knowingly. She made the necessary arrangements in a spare room. Father cut two pieces of thick wood to size, to support the plate, then started the process. Then he "asked" Mother to keep an eye on the apparatus, collect the soot every day, and replenish the oil in the lamp as required. The asking was, as it had always been, very polite. He always addressed Mother in the second person plural, but it never occurred to Mother that his request could be declined.

After twenty four hours the accumulated amount of soot was disappointingly minute. So Father, never one to admit defeat easily, started to use two more of our several kerosene-burning lamps, both very large this time. Four chairs were employed to support two large flat trays above the lamps. The sight of a regular ink factory right in my own house excited me no end. Mother looked sick, but managed a feeble smile at me. Soot production picked up. Father figured that in a week's time we should have enough soot for the first batch of first-quality home-made ink.

It wasn't practical in cold winter weather to keep the windows of the soot production room open. So it was with great reluctance that Mother entered the smoke-filled room every morning to replace the plates and run out. To the eight-year-old me, this daily trip to the soot factory was an event not to be missed, and I insisted on accompanying her. I would have stayed there longer to watch the process closely, but Mother kept the door locked. A few of the kids on the block were also fascinated by the idea, and came home with me one day to visit the factory. Mother wouldn't hear of it, fearing what neighbors would think of her, and of our house. The kids tried to peek through the windows, an attempt doomed to failure due to the thick smoke in the factory. Thus they had to be satisfied with my colorful description of the goings-on.

Fortunately for Mother, the messy job of refilling the kerosene chambers of the lamps had to be done only once, before Father decided at last that the soot supply was sufficient.

She spent two days cleaning the apparatus and the walls of the room. The ceiling could not be cleaned easily. It had to wait for the spring. Having had the Arabian gum ground and ready, Father went to work right away. He enlisted my enthusiastic help for mixing the ingredients well and stirring the juice vigorously before sifting it through a large rag. By the evening of the full day of joint work he was happy to declare the task accomplished.

The bottling was easy. Seven or eight large bottles, of the kind usually used for storing lemon juice by Mother, were filled with the fresh product and securely placed on a shelf. The array looked much like the contents of a cabinet in one of my friends' home, where the master of the household kept a dozen or so full bottles of his doctor-recommended dark red wine. I did not mention the resemblance to Father, because I knew that he would not like my frequenting a house whose master's doctor could recommend such medicines.

The next morning, in daylight, Father and I tested the finished product while Mother was making tea. We considered our lettering on the paper carefully and exchanged puzzled looks, aware without a word spoken that the results should be kept secret from Mother for as many minutes as possible. When Mother brought us breakfast and asked me how it was going with my ink test, Father answered for me. "It is quite legible," he said with great conviction and changed the subject. Mother didn't pursue the matter any further. She didn't need to. What was hidden from Mother's eyes was an almost invisible wet outline of letters on each of our sheets of paper. If it weren't for the sporadic dark dots of soot fastened to the paper along each letter, thanks to the Arabian gum in the concoction, Father's overstatement of the results of our efforts would be little more than a shocking lie.

Father's preoccupied look for the ensuing couple of days was a clear indication to Mother that the ink factory's mission was still unfulfilled. "We'll have to reduce the ink," he said on the next weekend morning, right after breakfast. He tested his proposed method by pouring the contents of the first bottle of ink into a pan and boiling it. We ended up with a considerably more visible but also more sticky product. This was proclaimed the official ink of the household until the next summer, when the weather would permit the employment of a better and more economical method for processing the rest of the stock. Father was sure that placing the raw ink in large, shallow trays and exposing it to direct summer sunlight, a more gradual and slow approach to the reduction phase of the production, would yield ideal results. After all, wasn't this the very method Mother used every summer to prepare our yearly supply of tomato paste?

"Where on earth did you buy this ridiculous ink?" asked my bench-mate in school as soon as he saw my first homework done with the new product. I hadn't thought of the inevitable question. "I don't know where my father got it," I lied. He and a couple of other classmates always seemed to have a way of asking uncomfortable questions. Although I never considered my family poor, everyone in class was aware that these three kids came from rich families. They had once asked each other and me, how often each kid's household had rice with lamb *khuresh* for supper. Now the kids whose families could afford it, had this expensive delicacy once a week, almost invariably on the weekends, except when they were entertaining dinner guests, of course. Taken aback by their disturbing answers to the frequency question, all ranging between three and five times a week, I had felt an overwhelming urge to suppress the truth. "Three times," I had said, choosing the minimal answer to preserve my family's dignity.

Several of my classmates, to whom my mother referred as the less fortunate ones, didn't seem to have nearly as big a dignity problem as I did. Even when scolded publicly by the vice-principal of the school for a delay in paying the monthly school fees, even when sent home and told not to come back without the fees owed, their faces didn't redden – and I envied them for it. These students did not ask hard questions about my ink. They must have assumed, naturally, that my father had found a new and more reasonable stationery store. One of them simply asked me, discreetly for my sake, to get the address of the evidently very affordable store from my father. "No need for the address," I said, not wanting to spread the rumor about the underground factory that had, in the course of a single day, become a source of embarrassment. "I have a lot of it; I'll bring you some."

When I was filling a small bottle with home-made ink to take to my classmate, Mother seemed much more pleased with my charitable act than I thought I deserved. I would only learn of the full reason much later. Meanwhile, I told the class snobs that my father was definitely not going back to this fraudulent ink-seller. A week or so later, Father encountered his own problem with his product. I could tell as soon as he came home one evening, cursing tax office tellers for refusing to accept a form he had carefully filled, using the new ink. "Perfectly legible," he kept telling us, "and these illiterates can't read it." He couldn't believe their impertinence. "After all, this was just a stupid tax form," he added, "and not a sample of calligraphy to be proudly exhibited on the walls of their guest rooms." I tried to use the opportunity to get him to buy some acceptable ink. He was still too proud to admit failure, but I didn't detect much conviction in his tone when he made promises about the far superior product planned for the coming summer. Mother winced.

As summer approached, Mother worried about the imminent ink-enhancing operation. "What would the visiting neighbors think?" she asked herself and me. She didn't ask Father. "Tell them we are making ink," he would have replied if asked, pretending not to understand why the question had to be asked at all. But his enthusiasm was clearly ebbing, a signal to Mother that she could perhaps do something about the looming summer humiliation.

Arriving home from school for lunch one day, I found Mother boiling the contents of all the remaining bottles of raw ink in one of the biggest pots we owned, the one used for boiling rice for very large dinner gatherings. She gave me my lunch, not sitting for lunch herself. "Not a word to your father about this," she said, "I have to finish this before he comes home this evening." She laughed when I said that I had hoped for better quality in the promised sun-reduced ink. She also promised me that I would never have to use the stupid ink beyond the current supply. "Just wait and see," she said mischievously, when she sensed that I didn't quite believe her.

No mention of ink was made until we exhausted our first batch of homemade ink. Father bought some regular, commercial ink. He said that waiting for the summer was preferable to using the inferior stove-top method for reduction. Mother and I knew that we had to change the subject and wait. The next time the home-made ink question came up, Mother gathered all her courage to say the one thing that she hoped would put an end to the discussion without injuring Father's pride, and pave the way for resumed consumption of normal, commercial ink in the household: "I gave it all to the less fortunate," she reported.

NO LONGER IMPOLITE TO CHEW GUM

"WE WOULD LIKE A PACKAGE OF *ADAMS*, PLEASE," I said to the clerk in the rather exclusive food and candy shop, called *Yusuf's Gastronomy*. "We" consisted of me and my schoolmate Rashid, both about ten years old. Rashid was accompanying me for more than just moral support. He had a stake in the intended transaction. He and I had saved most of our pocket money from the preceding three weeks. We desperately wanted chewing gum. Not just any chewing gum. American chewing gum. The cheap, traditional gum, obtainable for a mere fraction of a day's allowance, wouldn't do. It seemed to us that anyone who could possibly afford it, was buying and chewing the fashionable, neatly wrapped, imported American adams. Nobody dared to insult the fancy new treat in public by calling it "gum;" doing so would now be a definite indication of a gum-chewer's low class.

"Adams" happened to be the brand name of the first American gum sticks that appeared in Iran during the Forties. So it became, quite conveniently, the generic name for the sought-after product. (Several years later, I wouldn't be surprised to learn that older people in the city of Shiraz used the word "*charlie*" both as a noun and as a verb to refer to dry-cleaning, because the first modern establishment to provide this service in Shiraz had been called Charlie, to take advantage of the immense popularity of the Chaplin movies at the time.)

Rashid and I had experienced our first exciting taste of adams a month earlier, when a wealthier classmate of ours, who was in possession of a whole pack consisting of five sticks, let us break and share a stick between the two of us. After that experience, it was easy for us to decide never to touch the old stuff again. "Where did you get it?" I asked our generous friend. "Yusuf's Gastronomy;" he informed us, "the only place in the city that sells it; and it is three *gruns* each," he added, to demonstrate just how generous he had been. Very substantial price, indeed, I thought to myself, but everything good was unaffordable as a general rule. On the way home from school that day, Rashid and I, having agreed that our need for adams was irrepressible, proceeded to discuss the details of a possible plan for acquiring some.

My mother always allowed traditional gum chewing so long as I didn't let my father catch me in the act. But it was my father who tightly controlled the allotment of pocket money. According to him, all gum chewing was impolite. Rashid's parents didn't disapprove of the activity, but declared that "gum is gum, call it what you will." Explicitly asking for a special grant from our parents for the purpose of purchasing adams was thus out of the question.

"Adams is not that expensive, really," Rashid said, having reflected further on the matter, "and if we save our money for a few weeks, we'll be able to buy a whole pack for three gruns." Considering that we would be able to get five sticks –

five half-sticks for each of us – we prepared ourselves to save most of our pocket money for the next three weeks.

There was another catch: Yusuf's Gastronomy wasn't an ordinary grocery store of the kind our families frequented. Yusuf , a "half-Russian" by reputation, sold extra-ordinary things like foreign cheeses, pork sausages, vodka, wine, and beer. Would it be permissible by the Tenets of the Faith, Rashid and I wondered, to buy anything from this unclean store? "I could find out," I said to Rashid, " my father will know the answer." I assured him that I wouldn't ask direct questions about adams, of course.

I was pretty sure that one was permitted to buy dry goods even from an infidel if the goods themselves were not forbidden by the Tenets. I knew from experience that if Yusuf, or anybody working in his Gastronomy came to my house, they would be considered guests of dubious faith. When such a visitor was served, say, a cup of tea, Father would instruct Mother to "be careful with the cup," after the guest left. This meant that the cup had to be given a ritual washing to cleanse it: we either immersed it in a sufficiently large body of clean, clear water, or washed it three times by pouring water on it from an *aftafa,* a sort of elongated watering can with the sprinkler head removed. I also knew that if I shook hands with such a guest and if one of the hands involved in the shaking was wet or sweaty, then my hand would have to be cleansed the same way. To be absolutely sure, I decided to ask Father a theoretical question. Father liked such queries about everyday applications of the dictates of the Faith. "Assuming that we need a certain *halal* food item," I started putting the question to Father, "and assuming that this item is not sold in the stores owned by the faithful ..." Father immediately made the indicated assumptions and answered the obvious question. "Yes, of course," he said, "you could buy it from a *Kafir*, provided that the object was dry and was not, as far as you knew, handled by the store-keeper's possibly wet hands.

Thus it was that Rashid and I, having made sure of the permissibility of the proposed purchase, and having accumulated the considerable sum of three gruns between us for the purpose, were now face to face with the clerk at Yusuf's Gastonomy. I had all our money in my pocket – six half-grun coins, which could have bought us six tiny servings of ice cream during the previous three weeks. Rashid and I had no doubt that our big sacrifice, forgoing the ice cream and saving the money for adams, was well justified. We didn't ask the clerk about the price; we knew it. We were also aware that in this modern store one didn't haggle about prices. The clerk, having been informed of our intention, walked toward a special shelf covered with glass, and came back dutifully with a little shiny pack of adams that looked exactly like the one we so fondly remembered from our shared experience.

"Sorry," the clerk said as soon as I confidently placed the six half-grun coins on the counter, "but we don't sell adams sticks separately; you'll have to buy the whole pack of five sticks for fifteen gruns." Rashid and I exchanged quick, embarrassed glances. "We'll come back," Rashid said apologetically. I put the six coins back in my pocket. We left Yusuf's Gastronomy without acknowledging our error. Then we spotted the nearest ice cream vendor with his hand-driven cart. We ran to him and asked for double orders of the miniature ice cream servings to console ourselves. We reflected first on our huge misunderstanding of the price quoted by our generous friend, and then on the wealth of his family, which was evidently of much higher order than we had previously imagined.

On the way home, we met Rashid's cousin Massood, slightly older than us, who inquired about the cause of our obvious distress. We took him into our confidence. "You know," Massood began to respond with the kind of authority to which his seniority entitled him, "there is another way." We were immediately interested, of course. "Buy an American Army can," he said. We knew what he was talking about. These were sealed tin cans, each containing a ration of food items and other necessities, originally meant for combat-time consumption by the armed forces, acquired from American Army Surplus facilities somewhere, which were now sold by vendors in the street corners of Tabriz. You didn't know exactly what a can contained until you paid for it and opened it. It was a sort of grab-bag lottery. A father in my neighborhood had recently treated us kids to orange juice made with the powder found in one of those cans.

"But there was no adams in my neighbor's can," I protested. "It must have been a green can;" Massood asserted with no hesitation and with even more authority, "buy an orange one." He then named a few of his lucky friends who struck adams in orange cans. The going rate for an American Army can, green or orange, seemed to be set for the whole city: five gruns. Massoud was willing to be partners with us. Given about a week, he said, he'd be able to contribute the whole balance of two gruns to the common pot, if

Rashid and I promised to replenish our principal back to its pre-ice-cream sum of three gruns. We did.

Following Massood's advice presented mixed results. The orange-colored American Army can the three of us invested in did not produce any adams, but it contained, among other things, mostly forgettable, two packs of very appetizing chocolate – another sought-after treat. It was tentatively suggested that we sell the candy to raise money for another orange can. This was unanimously rejected after a thorough consideration of the odds involved. We resigned to the foreseeable adamsless future, but concentrated on enjoying our chocolate.

I would become adams-rich soon and unexpectedly: just a few months after the failed transactions, my older brother, now living in Tehran, sent me what I now remember as dozens of packs of adams. I couldn't believe my luck. (I would find out, years later, what had made this bounty possible. The clerk at the Gastronomy, who happened to know my brother, had told him about my quest for adams.) I could now afford to give a few packs – whole packs, not sticks – to Rashid and Massood. Remembering the generosity of my rich classmate, I offered him a pack too. "Fake adams," he said after he thanked me, unwrapped a stick, and started to chew it. "Look at the inner wrap," he instructed me, "any fool can tell it is made in Tehran." He conceded, though, that the taste was quite tolerable.

Yusuf's store eventually reduced the price of genuine adams. But it was too little and too late. Domestic entrepreneurs invaded the bazaar with their own newly developed, mass-produced versions of adams. Many and varied brand names filled the billboards on the shop walls. The beautifully wrapped "rooster-brand" dominated the domestic market. Our teachers still frowned if they caught us chewing adams in the school yard and punished us for committing the offence in class, but the activity ceased to be considered low-class. Even a teacher of English in a local school, who had recently visited the United States in an exchange program, was seen engaged in the activity while walking in the city park, but this wasn't surprising. "What do you expect?" offered my proper and pious neighbor, Lady Saria, "they go to *Amirga* for just six months, and what they learn is to either chew gum or whistle in the street, to keep a pet dog at home, and to read while in the washroom."

A lot of young people were now chewing something all the time. Nobody dared to do it in the presence of my father. Was he the only one left thinking that gum-chewing was categorically impolite? To Rashid's father, gum was still gum, whatever you called it. The original American adams, still quite expensive, continued to be preferred by the well-to-do-and-with-it. Rashid and I frequently spotted the teenaged daughters of the *à la mode* family, who lived next to our school, strolling in their modern dresses, accompanied by their governess, and chewing adams, undoubtedly the genuine American brand. A couple of our friends claimed that they could tell by the aroma surrounding any adams chewer whether the content of the mouth was domestic or imported. We chose not to believe them while we enjoyed our rooster-brand adams. "Adams is adams," Rashid declared to my total agreement, "call it what you will."

THE ARDUOUS PATH TO MY FIRST MOVIE

MY FAVORITE COUSIN, *AYAHYA*, PROMISED ME, when I was eight years old, that he would take me to see my first movie. This was exciting news. My father didn't allow such frivolities. My elder brother was a little younger than Ayahya, and, as I would learn much later, did go to movies unbeknownst to Father. But he didn't dare to risk Father's wrath by taking me along.

Ayahya was now in the Military College, training to be an officer. Before he moved to his college residence, and after losing his parents in Istanbul, he had lived with us for several years. This athletic, good-humored, kind, and generous addition to Father's drab and austere dominion was a godsend. When he was just a high school student with very meagre income, he frequently managed to buy little toys for me and even for my best friend Mamadali. As I grew older, I would also come to admire his independent ways. Although very deferential to his guardian uncle, he did not feel obligated to abide by those of Father's strict rules that made little sense to "normal" people. He broke them discreetly, but without fear. Against Father's absolute prohibition of all musical instruments, for example, he owned a winding gramophone, which he had brought back from

Istanbul. Usually well-hidden in his room, the sinful instrument would come out only when Father wasn't home. Thus it provided a great source of pleasure for the family on week days after school. His joining the Army Cadets, a move that was frowned upon by Father, but not quite forbidden, was another act of defiance. I am certain that this choice of school and career would have been out of the question in my brother's case. But Father made more allowances for his orphaned nephew than for his own children. I suppose he respected the fact that Ayahya's deceased father, a modern man compared to Father, would have consented.

Mamadali and I were often taken to the city park by Ayahya or by Mamadali's father who was slightly older than Ayahya. My father had no objections to these outings, and in fact he himself took me to the park sometimes. When he did, I was allowed to ride the merry-go-round, but not the Ferris-wheel, which was "too dangerous." He would also never buy me one of those delicious-looking cookies in various animal forms, which were wheeled around the park by street vendors; they were "too unclean." Nor would he get me any ice cream; the cream in summer time was "too risky, health-wise." In winter, incidentally, nobody sold or bought ice cream in Tabriz; so this meant no ice cream, ever. When Mamadali and I went to the park with his father or Ayahya, on the other hand, we did all those forbidden things. We didn't tell Father, and we didn't tell Mamadali's grandmother, Saria Khanum. She was even more strict than Father. In fact, going to the park was wrong according to her. "Taking a mere walk in that park is a sin," Saria Khanum maintained, because the former Shah of Iran "desecrated an old cemetery by converting it to this public park, where people carelessly trample on the remains of the departed faithful, may their souls all rest in peace."

The movie promise, which had so delighted me, was not to be fulfilled soon. Ever since Ayahya was admitted to the Military College, he was able to come home only on weekends. With Father also home, it wasn't easy to find an excuse to leave home long enough to see a movie. An opportunity would not present itself for a year or so. Meanwhile, my friends kept reporting on the movies they were seeing. "I go to the movies every single weekend," claimed one, during a boasting session in the school yard. "He is lying," whispered another in my ear, "his family can't afford that." A third student was more vocal. "But aren't there only three movie theatres in the whole city of Tabriz?" he asked with disbelief and envy. "And don't the movies run for several months each?" he went on. "Of course," agreed the fortunate kid, "and I get to see some of them several times." Of course, I repeated to myself, glad that I wasn't the one who had raised the obviously stupid question.

On the way to school every day, I saw the theatre billboards advertising their current movies. To have the widest possible appeal, they filled the board with as many different descriptive nouns about the movie as they could come up with. I didn't quite understand everything they said, but it seemed to me that they invariably billed every movie as "a story of love, fidelity, generosity, conflict, betrayal, hypocrisy, crime, revenge, honor, pride, patriotism, war, and more." To their credit, the movie advertisers hadn't yet acquired the habit of calling every movie "the best in the history of

Cinema." My friends showed particular interest in the movies that included a lot of fighting scenes between people and animals, which often meant Tarzan movies and wild Westerns. Grownups seemed to favor Indian or Egyptian productions awash in song and dance. All the movies were in foreign tongues. Domestically produced imitations, with the added language advantage were still a few years in the future. Since the story lines were usually not completely understood by most of the audiences anyway, the theatres sometimes performed cut-and-paste operations on their reels to attract customers. I realized this when the message on one of the billboards was amended in huge letters: "Hurry! Hurry! Many Belly Dance Scenes Added!"

Mamadali and I learned from an older boy how to make a cheap "movie theatre." My old house had quite a few abandoned rooms surrounding a spacious courtyard. Fifty years before my time, the house had belonged to a well-to-do landowner and had contained several "suites" for his frequent guests. Most of the suites were now in a state of disrepair, which made them suitable for unrestricted use by the kids. Mamadali and I were determined to convert one of the suites to a theatre. All we needed, we found, was a magnifying glass and some "*fillims*," which meant single frames cut off movie reels. We already had a few fillims. Kids loved these frames. They collected, bought, sold, exchanged, and bartered them, very much like baseball cards in North America. Tarzan fillims were among the more popular, but almost any frame with a clear picture of a famous "artist" was collectible, especially if it was a color fillim. Of course we would have to collect more fillims. This could be done gradually. But more pressing was the need for a magnifier. My father, then in his seventies, and Saria Khanum, in her sixties, owned their personal magnifying glasses for reading, but it was unthinkable that they would consider lending them to us. Our determination and self-discipline paid off: Mamadali and I saved most of our weekly allowances for many weeks that winter, and were able to purchase a magnifier in the spring, just in time for the summer showings in our "Cinema" to open soon.

We prepared one of the suites for this purpose and put a hand-made sign on it that said "Cinema Royal." (Most of the movie houses that advertised in the papers, especially those in Tehran, had fancy Western names: Cinema Metropol, Cinema Venus, Cinema Rex.) It wasn't hard to darken the suite. It had just one old window which we covered with layers of newspaper, except for a broken panel of glass. This we covered with a sturdy piece of cardboard on which we had carefully made a small rectangular hole just the size of a single fillim. We had a few old chairs in the suite, but we also fashioned more seats from large, empty kerosene cans and covered them with rags. My mother and Mamadali's good-natured great aunt, "Great Auntie" to every kid who knew her, watched our renovation efforts on the suite with amusement, pretending to believe in our movie-showing plans. Neither had ever seen a movie, of course, but both would have loved to, if their religious families had been a little more permissive. My father would have no objections to the goings-on in the courtyard, and would dismiss our earnest attempts as child-play, so long as they didn't interfere with my very rigid schedule of training in calligraphy,

Father's favorite art form. Saria Khanum, on the other hand, would not be so easy to deal with if she ever found out about our unholy aspirations. Fortunately for us, she was almost never around and always busy with her religious gatherings that were usually held in far-away districts of the city.

On the first sunny day that followed the preparation of the theatre, Cinema Royal was ready for a test. The boy who taught us the art of movie showing had the convenience of electric power in his house. My father was opposed to electricity on the obvious grounds that it was too dangerous. But we knew from our extensive research into the matter, and after consultations with another boy with a home-made cinema, how to deal with this short-coming. Which is why we had to have sunshine. We borrowed a mirror from Mother and rested it on a rock in the sunny side of the courtyard so that it reflected the rays on the covered window, right where the fillim hole was. A Tarzan fillim had already been fitted into the hole, upside down. So when we entered the suite, closed the door, and I held the magnifier in front of the fillim and adjusted its distance, a beautiful, large, color picture of Tarzan himself miraculously appeared on the opposite wall.

Having tested Cinema Royal so successfully, we immediately invited Mother and Great Auntie for a viewing. They were too curious to hesitate in accepting. We ushered them in and seated them in our best cushioned chairs. As soon as I closed the door, Mamadali noticed something terribly wrong: the small source of light from the hole had disappeared. "Bear with us," we begged of the friendly audience, trying not to panic. Unfriendly audiences in movie houses were notoriously demanding, if our movie-going classmates were to be believed. Only recently, unsatisfied spectators in Cinema Diana were reported to have thrown corncobs at an incompetent projectionist. Mamadali and I ran out to the mirror on the far side of the courtyard and discovered that by adjusting its position we could get the patch of reflected light back on the fillim hole. To the delight of everybody present, the glorious image of Tarzan was once again projected on the white wall of Cinema Royal. Mother and Great Auntie were truly impressed. This was the closest thing to a real movie Great Auntie would ever see. Mother would see her first movie ten years later, at my insistence and only while away from Tabriz. "What would the neighbors think," she would wonder, "if they saw Haj Abbas Ali's wife in a movie house?" This even after Father was long gone.

There was this annoying little problem with the moving reflection from the mirror. It took Mamadali and me another day to find out that it wasn't the mirror that was moving as a result of our negligence in securing it properly. "It is the sun!" my older brother informed us condescendingly, when he paid a visit to Cinema Royal. "And the reflection moves when the sun does," he said, "and you can't adjust the sun." Thus it was decided, in the interest of smooth operation, that one of us should stay out of the theatre, whenever a show was in progress, and keep adjusting the mirror. With all the minor problems now resolved, we were proud to arrange a late afternoon showing for Ayahya, on one of his weekend leaves from the Military College. "We'll go to a real movie soon," he assured me again when he was leaving Cinema Royal, "as soon as I can arrange it."

Now there remained only one problem to be solved, but it was a major one: how to enhance our meager fillim repertory. We dreamed of instituting an admission charge of two pennies, but nobody would pay that to view just a dozen fillims. So we admitted the neighborhood kids in exchange for lending us fillims from their personal collections. We didn't find this satisfactory and looked for alternatives. "I know where to buy good fillims," said an older neighbor kid one day, "and I can take you there if you have the money." Mamadali and I took all the change we had and followed him to another district of the city. We were a little scared when we arrived at the abandoned cemetery, where the teen-aged fillim dealers were busy "shooting walnuts," a variation of shooting marbles for money. They invited our guide to join in. He declined. They threw curious glances at Mamadali and me. "What is the hurry?" asked the oldest walnut shooter, when informed about our business mission. "Stay a while and take a look at our choice Tarzan fillims," he said, addressing our obvious chief negotiator, "and I'll give the little ones free fillims if they are nice to me." Our leader got red in the face. The three of us knew we had to run out of the cemetery as fast as we could.

We were fortunate to find a more benign source of fillims in a hat shop in the bazaar that specialized in *casquettes*. These were the regulation hats required, by the Department of Education, for all male students of first through twelfth grades. A few of our rich schoolmates had their casquettes made by their fathers' tailors, but almost every student bought his compulsory hat from one of the three or four shops in the city that mass-produced them. The hat was made of purple-black wool except for visors and sweat bands. The material used for the sweat bands consisted, invariably, of recycled remnants of worn movie reels, which the city theatres sold in bulk to the hat makers. Our casquette-maker in the bazaar had a second occupation on the side: he was a whole-sale dealer in bags made of old newspapers. Mamadali and I offered him a mutually profitable deal: we would make bags for him in return for individual frames cut off his reels. The summer was ending, and with the school year and high season for casquette sales approaching, his hands, as well as his two sons', were full with hat production. "All right," he readily agreed, pointing to a big load of newspapers in the corner of the stores, "you take them home, bring me the bags you make, and I'll save you fifty choice fillims." Having examined the sweat bands in our own worn hats, we knew that all the frames in the band of a single casquette were almost identical, so we explained to him that he should cut each frame off a reel only after several sweat bands were produced. He said he knew exactly what we wanted. Evidently, he had already concluded other transactions with fillim fans.

One morning, when both Father and Saria Khanum were gone for the day, Mamadali and I enlisted the help of Mother and Great Auntie to turn all the newspapers from the hat shop into assorted bags, using up the glue supply in my house. We dried the bags in the sun, and we didn't answer the door until we had bundled them up neatly and hidden them in Cinema Royal. Mother and Great Auntie, forever protective of the remnants of their once-upper-class dignity, wouldn't want any callers to see the assembly line.

True to his promise, the casquette-maker had the fifty fillims, not any two of them too much alike, ready for us when we delivered the bags. He liked the bags, and gave us a few extra frames. We all enthusiastically agreed that we'd do business again. On the way back to Cinema Royal, delighted with the prospect of the new shows, Mamadali and I dreamed of the illustrious future of our theatre. Perhaps, we thought, we'd be able to show really moving pictures some day. The impending school year interrupted our dreams. And by the start of the next summer, we came to regard the whole enterprise as a little childish.

Having been constantly reminded by me of his big promise, Ayahya took advantage of an infrequent occasion on which Father would be absent from home on a Wednesday evening, to attend some important gathering of his old friends. Ayahya found a pretext and asked for a few hours of leave from his Military College residence. "Don't take your shoes off," Ayahya said to me, when I came home from school on that Wednesday, "we are going right away." My first movie was about to become a reality. We knew that Father would go to his gathering directly from the bazaar, where he worked, and would be absent for several hours. But Mother still seemed a little nervous about the whole idea. Ayahya had to assure her that we would be home long before Father could possibly get back.

We started toward the theatre. I wished Ayahya were not in such a big hurry. I wanted to be seen, going to the movies, by more friends who happened to be playing in the street. But why was Ayahya running? Were we late for the movie? No, he said, but kept watching over his shoulders.

The reason for his haste became clear when a military policeman stopped him, and asked for his reason to be out of residence in the middle of the week. Ayahya showed him some papers and said that he was taking his cousin to the doctor. The man didn't seem to believe this until Ayahya convinced him by tactfully putting a small bill in his palm. This movie was going to be very costly, I figured.

Without further incident we reached the theatre. The red lit plate above the ticket kiosk informed us that "Act Two" was in progress. That didn't matter, of course; we couldn't afford the luxury of waiting for the next sitting. Few people did anyway. You could buy your ticket, enter the theatre, and leave whenever you wanted. Some customers would sit through two or more consecutive showings of a movie if they particularly liked it. (Just a few years later, I would hear of a young man in Tehran who fell desperately in love with Silvana Mangano once he saw her beautiful peasant-girl image in the Italian neo-realist movie, Bitter Rice. He did not miss a single showing of the movie afterwards. He would go every afternoon and change seats after each showing to give both Silvana and himself different vantage points in the hope that Slivana's eyes would eventually meet his.) We paid for our tickets, followed the path shown us by an usher-bouncer's small flash light, and took our seats.

It was an American movie, I am sure. Nobody understood what was being said. It was no use even if one did speak English, the noise level in the theatre was so high. The audience waited for occasional interruptions of the movie by inserted screens on which only very partial script was given in Persian. This was read aloud and translated into

Azeri Turkish by the few fortunate enough to have the capability, for the benefit of their accompanying illiterate relatives. As soon as the movie resumed, so did the friendly chit-chat and the consumption of sandwiches and drinks the audience had brought along. Cigarette smoking never stopped. The excitement of just seeing a movie was enough for me, and I didn't mind the noise, the smoke, or the insufficient dialogue. I didn't even mind the flying sunflower seed shells that sporadically landed on me. They were discharged, not always inadvertently, from the balcony just above us, by loud groups of young men talking through mouthfuls of seeds in the process of being shelled.

The end of Act Two was signaled by the ringing of a bell and a brief intermission. When the lights went on, I looked around to spot any friends or acquaintances, who would later be able to attest to my presence at the movies, if the need arose. But I found Ayahya extremely agitated. "Get ready," he said as soon as the theatre darkened and Act Three started, "we have to leave." We hurried out, sped through several blocks, and entered a candy shop. Ayahya bought me some ice cream and explained apologetically that he had sighted one of his College superiors in the movie house, and that he was glad we got out before the officer could recognize him. We made it home with plenty of time before Father returned from his meeting.

Ayahya was transferred to Tehran a few weeks later. I would not see the inside of another commercial movie house for five years. But I didn't have to wait that long to see my first full motion picture. Only one year later, Reza, a wealthy classmate of mine invited me to his house for a private showing of a real movie. This was no less than a multiple miracle: I hadn't known that such a thing was possible in a private home; also, I hadn't expected his father to be so utterly different from all the other fathers, even the rich ones, whom I knew. And I hadn't dreamed of encountering such good luck.

"I got permission from my father," whispered Reza after school one day, "to invite you to see a Charlie Chaplin movie at our place." He must be joking, I thought. I had spent many hours in his house, one of my few destinations approved by Father. I had helped Reza with his homework for more than a year, and he wanted to do something for me in return. Still, I was puzzled. I had never seen any evidence of movie showing in his home. In fact, I knew that his father, like mine, did not permit him or any other member of his family to go to the movie theatres. "But you should remember," he warned, "that you are not supposed to tell anybody about it." His father, he emphasized, would be furious if this condition wasn't strictly adhered to, a circumstance which would certainly end our friendship. This was no problem for me, since I had already been privy to a more scandalous family secret of another friend whose father had bottles of medicinal wine in his study. Movies, after all, were not vehicles of sin by themselves. I was sure of this, because even Father never condemned them categorically; it was just that movie-going was potentially sinful. "But movies are not against our religion or anything," I said to my friend now, wondering why anybody would want to make a secret of such a privilege, instead of bragging about it. "No," he agreed, "but my father says he has to do business with a lot of people who wouldn't understand."

The Charlie Chaplin session in Reza's house, after almost a whole night of sleepless and excited anticipation, proved to be a revelation to me in more than one way. Having trusted me with one big secret already, the family had apparently decided to reveal another. I couldn't believe my eyes, when I entered the darkened family room, in which there were several short rows of chairs occupied by grown-up men and women, boys and girls. Extended family members and trusted friends, I presumed. Certainly not just the immediate family. But no woman was wearing a *chadra*; nor was there a curtain dividing the room into male and female quarters. In fact, men and women seemed to have been seated randomly, and women were freely talking to men. The Master of the house would have a lot to explain, I thought, if his business associates knew about such gatherings in his guest hall. I made a mental note to ask Reza later about this anomaly, given that his was known to be a God-fearing household. Then I settled in my seat and thoroughly enjoyed the silent story told in moving pictures. Was it the Gold Rush? I am not entirely sure.

After the movie, the guests adjourned to the reception area for refreshments. While I was enjoying my cake, the projectionist was paid for his services and whisked away, together with his substantial gear, in a horse-driven cab. I observed that the apparatus was carefully hidden in a dark bag. The host was, no doubt, mindful of his business associates. When I walked home that day, I felt like a new boy. I had witnessed a full picture in motion. I would talk to Reza, I decided, to see if his father would kindly include Mamadali the next time he invited me to see a movie in his house. Would it be at all possible, I wondered, for me to get Mother invited too, sometime, perhaps when they had a showing for women only. She would love it too, I knew.

"Do you always have mixed company in your house?" I asked Reza the next day. I told him how surprised I was by the goings-on, having thought that his father was a religious man. "Of course he is religious," Reza claimed, "and he never forgets to say his daily prayers." Then he informed me about *sigha,* a religious pact which I had heard of but knew very little about. I asked for enlightenment. "It is very simple," he said, offering me an example, "take my mother and our grown-up male neighbor, Mr. Shahab, who are not close relatives, right?" I nodded. "Mr. Shahab is not supposed to see my mother's face and hair, right?" he asked, defining the problem more clearly. "Yes, but only if Mr. Shahab is religious," I answered unnecessarily. "Well, he is as religious as my father," Reza said, "but there is a way to make it possible for a man and a woman to see each other and socialize freely without committing a sin." This was truly confusing to me. "It was simple," he said, starting to take obvious pleasure in furthering my education, "my father had a clergyman draw up a sigha pact between my baby sister and Mr. Shahab." This was definitely becoming more interesting. The clergyman had, with this pact, formally "wedded" the toddler to Mr. Shahab for an unspecified period of time. It was not a real marriage, he informed me, and would later be annulled with no fuss, no expense, and no consequences. It was just a technicality: Reza's mother was now Mr. Shahab's mother-in-law, and thus a close relative for all religious purposes. In particular, there was nothing sinful about her uncovered face in his presence.

My appeal for the inclusion of Mamadali on the next guest list for home movies did not succeed. Saria Khanum was considered just too much of a risk by Reza's family, should she ever find out. Mother would definitely not constitute a risk, but I decided not to ask Reza for an invitation: His parents were clearly not interested in segregating genders for social occasions. And Mother wouldn't understand. Even if she did, it was just too complicated. I didn't have a baby sister to marry Mr. Shahab.

MY BEST FRIEND MAMADALI AND I, aged about five and six respectively, were waiting impatiently for the short weekly pleasure ride on our favorite mule. It was a bright Thursday afternoon in the second full summer of World War Two, but the war wouldn't come to Iran for another month or two.

Ordinary folks in my district of the city took the neutrality of the country for granted. Those men who could read newspapers, and especially those rich and modern enough to own the newly imported magic box called radio, sometimes abstractly discussed world affairs. With the single exception of an army officer's wife, no grown-up woman on my block could read and write; some could read, but only their sacred books, without understanding a word. The children of Tabriz under twelve, unlike their elders, had not yet experienced a war or a riot.

While Mamadali and I waited for the mule to arrive in the outer courtyard of a neighbor, the neighborhood women, having gathered in the much larger inner courtyard, were getting ready for the arrival of the owner and rider of the mule, a cleric known by his informal but respectful name of Amirza Hasan. The occasion was the good women's weekly *marsia*, a periodic commemoration of tragic deaths of the Great Martyrs of the Faith in 680 A.D. During a marsia meeting the audience would listen to such preachers and singers of lamentations as Amirza Hasan, and then sob and wail along with the singer. Marsia sessions were of course segregated by gender. This gathering was for women only, who would, theoretically, prefer the sessions to be led by a female *marsia khan*, unfortunately a very rare specimen. Thus the women would usually have to settle for the male variety. This entailed for every participating adult the slight inconvenience of covering not only her body, but also her face and hair while a marsia khan was on duty. If one of us young kids, in an emergency, needed to speak to a mother or grandmother during a seance, we would face a problem: entering the large inner courtyard, which was elaborately prepared for the occasion, we would encounter fifty or sixty dark, small tent-like objects distributed uniformly all over the thickly carpeted floor. Inside each tent, actually a loose robe called a *chadra* or a *charshub*, depending on the style, there would be an invisible woman crying to the tune of the presiding singer. To distinguish them from each other, we kids would have to go by each tent's size and color or the sounds emanating from it. My mother did not usually attend marsias except on the holy occasions of the lunar year, but, as a neighborhood kid, I had the privilege of inclusion among the young hangers-on every Thursday afternoon.

The devout and relatively well-to-do household hosting the current gathering could afford to pay several marsia khans each week to lead the religious seances. The leading men came one at a time, more or less on schedule. They were first served tea and sweets in the outer courtyard by Mehdi, a young male member of the household (who, by virtue of his young age, was permitted to travel back and forth freely between the men and women in the house). After a brief rest, the marsia khan would proceed to the inner courtyard where the audience sat on the carpeted floor, and where he would occupy the solitary chair that was obviously reserved for the leader of the session. Each man had his own style, but always started with a soft, almost inaudible voice, saying prayers, as if to himself. If he thought of himself as a learned man, he would then deliver a short lecture on applying principles of the Faith to everyday issues concerning pious women and their families, but he knew what the main purpose of any marsia was. Accordingly, he would pick a suitable martyr of the Faith, male or female, and relate a version of his or her tragic story as recorded by some reliable source. The story-telling would gradually turn to loud singing and wailing. Not every kind of singing was permissible; no vibrato, for example, was to be included, according to the guidelines written by experts. "This is not a God-damned Russian opera," I once overheard an old expert say to one of his followers, commenting on an ignorant young marsia khan's sinful, pulsating rendition of a perfectly innocent lamentation. Minor transgressions on the part of the singing Marsia khans were, however, usually tolerated so long as they extracted a good, loud, collective sob from the audience.

Between consecutive sobbing sessions, after one marsia khan had left and the next had not yet arrived, members of the audience had ample time to uncover their heads and faces, wipe their eyes, rest, console each other, sip tea and nibble sweets, exchange news and gossip, and subtly eye the younger girls in the congregation as prospective brides for their sons and nephews. The kids would briefly interrupt their games outside and come into the room for treats. The only sombre part of these usually festive intermissions was when the women took a collection of money to help a neighbor in distress.

Amirza Hasan was an elderly man, looking dignified in his suit and hat when he arrived on his mule every Thursday afternoon. But he wasn't comfortable in the obligatory, Western-style suit which did not, in his view, befit a man of God. What he strongly preferred was the proper clergymen's attire – a special robe and a turban. Unfortunately, he was not allowed to wear that uniform in public; the ruling Shah of Iran at the time, in his sweeping modernization efforts, had strictly forbidden wearing the uniform for anybody other than a very few, fully certified high priests of the Faith. The resourceful Amirza Hasan was not satisfied with the easy solution to the problem found by practical younger marsia khans. These compromising new-comers simply sang and wept in street clothes; a few of them even traveled on bicycles. Not Amirza Hasan. He had taken to hiding the proper garments in a bag identical to the one in which a mule-rider would normally keep the mule's lunch of barley.

On this Thursday, he arrived a little late, and explained that he had to alter his route to avoid cruising policemen, who had, on the order of the Shah, become more vicious in enforcing street dress codes. He was caught and given a warning on a recent occasion when he had absent-mindedly left his turban on, and he was, as a result, afraid that they may be after him even in street clothes. Mehdi, Mamadali, and I said our respectful hellos to Amirza Hasan, which he answered with a kindly smile. Then he took his robe and turban from his mule-bag, donned them, and looked even more dignified. He sat down to sip his tea, helped himself to the sweets, thanked Mehdi, and indicated to him that it was okay for "the little ones" to have a brief supervised ride. He emphasized "supervised," because of the incident, a few weeks earlier, when I had managed to mount the mule un-assisted, and the mule had, to my extreme horror, taken off and traveled, at a speed that felt like lightning to me, all the way to its accustomed rest station in the little caravanserai adjoining the local bazaar. Fortunately, several shopkeepers in the bazaar, having recognized Amirza Hasan's mule, had helped me dismount and I had managed to run home be-fore they could also recognize me and squeal to my father. Chastened by that experience, I had no problems with be-ing supervised on this day's slow ride through the length of our narrow cul-de-sac and back. The whole ride must have taken less than five minutes, but it was a great joy for Mamadali and me as usual.

Amirza Hasan, having finished his session of marsia, and having accepted a prepared sealed envelope from Mehdi containing his fee, changed back to his street clothes, care-fully hid his robe and turban, and rode his mule out of the cul-de-sac. Mamadali and I said our polite farewells to him and rushed into the marsia court for more treats with the grown-ups. The mood of the congregation was different from before. Having heard of the reason for Amirza Hasan's uncharacteristic delay, the women were swapping their own horror stories of encounters with the police. "The cops seem to have multiplied recently;" a woman was saying, "no street corner is safe these days; just as I was walking here today, a cop took my scarf and destroyed it." The hostess offered to lend her a spare scarf for her walk back. Mamadali's grandmother, Saria, had more information to impart. "What makes it worse for Amirza Hasan," she reported, "is that his own son is a policeman." Sympathy for Amirza Hasan and indignation toward the stray son filled the courtyard air. Apparently, many of the women hadn't yet heard about the son's new, ungodly profession.

Ali, Amirza Hasan's youngest and most promising son, reportedly started to disobey him as soon as he entered ninth grade in school. Amirza Hasan had entertained high hopes for him as a budding man of cloth. He hoped that Ali would enter a seminary some day, study hard, and become such an indisputable scholar of the Faith, that even the Shah would not dare to order him out of his robe and turban. Alas, Ali started to have other ideas: he sang silly songs in a school play, he marched to the military-style school band in a procession to celebrate the Shah's birthday, and dreamed of becoming a police officer. Humiliated, Amirza Hasan watched his son, but did not take the step that his sterner colleagues would have taken. He did not take Ali out of school and force him to start a career as a wealthy man's clerk or accountant, for example. Instead, he just prayed for Ali and hoped he'd come to his senses one day.

Evidently, Ali had not yet come to his senses. We saw him occasionally in his police uniform riding his bike. Fortunately for Amirza Hasan, Ali was not assigned to our district, but everybody was sure that somewhere in Tabriz he was committing the sin of relieving pious women of their head-dresses or raiding an unsuspecting household holding a marsia session. Amirza Hasan and presumably the other members of his immediate family had, if the rumors could be trusted, stopped talking to him or about him. "What a waste" said one of the regular marsia participants upon hearing the news from Saria, "and such a tall, handsome, and polite boy he used to be too."

As soon as the old Shah abdicated in September of that year, and was exiled to far-away Johannesburg by the British forces occupying the country, all of his Westernization efforts came to an abrupt end. Old seminaries opened their doors again, and their staff and students, now vastly multiplied in numbers, wore their robes and turbans with a sense of pride and revenge. Nobody harassed properly covered women. Saria and her fellow-marsia-enthusiasts felt free to roam around the almost cop-free streets of Tabriz and hop from one marsia site to the next. The Russian soldiers, now very visible everywhere in Tabriz streets, seemed to be indifferent to them. The women looking for marsia sessions were guided in their quest by large black flags all over the city. Hitherto forbidden, the flags had just come out of their closets and were aggressively advertising the locations of the numerous houses hosting the holy singing meetings. Marsia sites for men even started to have loudspeakers installed outside, so passers-by wouldn't be completely deprived of the enjoyment of soul-cleansing songs and lamentations. In the mourning periods of the year, processions of men, clad in black, paraded in the bazaar, grouped according to their preferred method of self-flagellation; some thumping their chests, and some beating their bare backs with special steel chains, all in unison, to the tune of their own ferocious singing.

The most spectacular event I witnessed for the first time in my life, though, was reserved for that most sacred mourning occasion which occurred only once every 354 days, on the tenth day of the lunar year. On this day, some of the good men changed their black outfits to *kafans*, white sheets of cloth customarily used to wrap dead bodies in before burial. The men were rattling sharpened sabres, while singing devotional songs that got more and more devotional as noon approached. At high noon, the well-documented moment of the Great Martyrdom was celebrated by the brave mourners' spilling blood: their rattling sabres came down simultaneously on their prepared, clean-shaven heads, staining their kafans with an amount of blood proportional to each man's devotion. "Why wasn't I there to die with you and for you?" they chanted as their sabres cut into their heads repeatedly, "Do I deserve then to be alive after your selfless sacrifice for us?" I feared I was about to witness the violent death of some, if not all, of them. My older brother who had, unbeknownst to my parents, taken me to view this sacred parade, consoled me. "In all my life," he reassured me with his usual sarcastic smile, "I have never seen one of these people die; they are experts, they know how to do it so the wound would heal in a week." I didn't believe him. Suddenly I recognized the eight-year-old son of Qassem, the local grocer, among the kafan-clad men. He was wearing a mini-kafan, but did not have a sabre in hand. He was accompanying Qassem, who used his sabre gingerly to make a few small cuts on his son's shaven head as soon as he was done with his own. I would be reminded of this scene, even decades later, whenever a flight attendant instructed passengers that in an emergency they should attend to their children's oxygen masks only after their own.

"Weren't you scared?" I asked the grocer's son a few days later in school, confessing to him how scared I had been, even as a mere spectator. "No," he answered promptly and proudly, "it wasn't my first time either." He was happy to inform me that according to a solemn promise made to God by his father, the procedure would be repeated on the same occasion every year until he himself reached the responsible age of fourteen, at which time he could decide whether or not to continue the ritual with a sabre of his own. "Besides," he said, "my father told me that if anybody dies from the wound of a sabre on this day, he is counted among the martyrs himself and goes directly to paradise." Mamadali and I were further enlightened on the matter by his aunt, "Great Auntie" to me as well as to him. "Qassem the grocer and his wife were worried about not having a son after she produced seven daughters in a row;" she said, "so he made this promise to God in return for a son." Promises to God had to be kept , of course, so Mamadali and I were grateful to our parents for not having negotiated such ominous pacts with the Almighty on our behalf. True, Mamadali was subjected to periodic blood letting for "medical" reasons under his grandmother Saria's supervision, but that is another story.

I was determined to ask Father about the head-splitters' procession. I was still frightened by the experience, but I didn't want Father to know that I had seen it with my own eyes. Fortunately, my baby-sitter's young husband, who always brought his spiritual enquiries to Father, visited Father one early morning and asked the burning question in my presence. He wanted to know about the religious merits of "head blood-letting," as he put it. Was he perhaps considering a sacred pact with God, in quest of a baby boy? "No merits at all," said Father, to my utter surprise and relief, "on the contrary, this act, like any other act causing bodily harm to yourself or others, is against all principles of our Faith." The visitor, knowing how strictly religious Father was, couldn't believe his ears. "Why don't our experts, our sources of emulation, say something to the public about it, then?" he asked. "Because," said Father without hesitation, "they are afraid of the mob, especially when it comes to curbing the mob's excited demonstrations of love and devotion toward our beloved martyrs."

I would remember this uncharacteristically bold expression of Father's opinion decades after his death – while attempting to deconstruct his life. Reflecting on this memory, I would find a likely resolution to an important puzzle: why did he go through all that trouble of traveling to the holy city of Najaf in the mid 1880s and study theology only to quit a year later and become a businessman? I knew that he had taken this perilous journey when he was eighteen years old, on a donkey and accompanying a caravan of merchants for safety. Just getting there from his home town of Salmas, had taken six months. The official excuse offered by him for quitting was an abrupt "change of mind." Fat chance, I always thought. My oldest brother figured that Father had differences of opinion with his mentors in the Najaf schools of higher learning. But why didn't he change his mentors (instead of changing his mind, which was always so difficult for him)? Surely, there was an abundance of mutually differing approaches to matters theological in the learned Shiite circles of the late nineteenth-century Najaf? Thus I would find a partial explanation, at least a hypothesis : he was afraid of the mobs he would have to confront if he ever became an authority and a source of emulation.

A year after my family moved out of my childhood house adjoining Mamadali's, Saria came to take my mother to a special marsia session in another district of Tabriz. She stopped for tea. I had seen her and Mamadali frequently even after we moved, but she asked me to come and sit in the guest room and talk to her. "This is goodbye," she said to me, "I want us to see each other for one last time, to our hearts' content." I was puzzled for a brief moment, but then she proceeded to explain herself. Although I was still not an official adult at the age of thirteen, not yet passed into the zone of "responsibility," she wanted to be on the safe side. "Starting next time we meet," she announced, "I'll be covering my face in your presence." I should have expected this, of course, but I still found it hard to accept my imminent transformation from her grandson's best friend – possibly the only friend Saria approved of, the only one for whom she could be said to have a soft spot in her heart – to just another strange man. Not only would I not see her face again, I might seldom hear her voice if she decided to treat me as a true stranger, and hence talk to me only when absolutely necessary.

When a week later, during the same mourning month, my mother accompanied Saria to the same special marsia site, I was curious. "What is so special?" I inquired, "Surely there are enough marsia sessions held in our own neighborhood to last you for the whole month." The center of attraction, it turned out, was Ali, the former police agent, Amirza Hasan's estranged son. "Ali has repented," Saria happily informed me – and I was glad that she was still talking to me, albeit through her charshub – "God be praised. He resigned from the police force right after the evil Shah's abdication and entered the seminary. Amirza Hasan is so pleased to see him in robe and turban." My mother was also enthusiastic about the performance of the young, born-again singer of lamentations. "He has such a strong, rich voice," she put in, "he is destined to be one of the most popular marsia khans in town."

The purists complained a little about "*Ajan* Marsia Khan." (The first word in the title, a form of "agent" borrowed from French, meaning "policeman" was an endearing nickname given to Ali by the good women of Tabriz, to indicate his old profession and thus his new enlightened post-penitence status.) The nit-pickers had trouble with the occasional vibrations detected in his otherwise acceptable singing voice. But Ali's new-found faith, his sincere atonement, his passionate rendering of the Great Martyrs' stories in verse, and his undeniable popularity silenced them, at least for the time being. His above-average fees allowed him to hire a horse-driven cab, a *phaeton*, to travel between his many marsia destinations. Amirza Hasan himself, as serene as ever, a lot more comfortable now in his old brown robe and white turban, was still seen riding his mule. I occasionally met him in the old neighborhood and exchanged strictly man-to-man greetings with him, hiding my nostalgia for the mule rides of yore.

Just a few years later, the mule was on its way out as a means of personal transportation for most people. Even the phaeton was starting to leave the scene to make room for the motorized taxi cab. The popular Ajan Marsia Khan got married, thereby disappointing all but one of the match-makers among his congregation. His fees went up, and he rode taxis from one marsia destination to the next, but there were disconcerting rumors. "The way his wife dresses is not quite suitable for a woman in a clergyman's household," opined a neighbor of Saria's, who had accompanied her on a short visit to my mother. To be sure, the young wife did cover her hair in public, but she also did something she didn't have to do, now that the ill-fated Shah's dress codes were all but forgotten: she was sighted in the street wearing a regular overcoat rather than a *charshub*. "But that is not all," reported Saria's well-informed companion, "I heard that Ali himself sang a song on the radio recently." Her household, like other ultra-pious women's, did not permit a radio set, by now affordable and quite common among middle-class citizens of Tabriz. "I heard it from a reliable source," she said.

Ali's singing on the radio was confined to sacred occasions and consisted of the same lamentations as those sung in marsia gatherings. The Government at the time was busily courting the clergy and promoting marsias. "This is certain to turn the old Shah in his grave;" said a secular newspaper columnist, "must we undo everything done by the late king, even all the good things he did? Must we promote superstition?" Qassem the grocer was all for the current Government policy and offered free tea to those customers who lingered a while to listen to the popular marsia khan on the shop's loud radio. Saria was not impressed by the official pro-piety noises. "You can't be sincere broadcasting marsia in the afternoon and dance music in the evening," she maintained. "What the Government radio is doing is of vital necessity," declared an editorial in a fiercely anti-communist newspaper, "we need more of these praiseworthy programs to fight all the subversive forces so well-hidden amongst us."

The singing of lamentations on the radio, even the occasional vibrations in Ali's voice, broadcast all over the place, didn't cause too many raised eyebrows, but a widely circulating rumor did. Unconfirmed reports had him singing at private parties to the accompaniment of instrumental music. "And not nice songs either," elaborated one of Saria's informants, "no, it was one of those vulgar songs that lead our idle youth astray." Damning information indeed. "May the Almighty protect all of us from the ever-present temptations." Saria prayed. This wasn't all; some of these parties were reported to have taken place in disreputable households, like that of the Provincial Tax Bureau chief who was known to drink his vodka openly. "This would be the end of Ajan Marsia Khan as a man of God," agreed the good men and women of our district. And the prophecy seemed to prove accurate soon. To the chagrin of the old Amirza Hasan and his wife, once again on the verge of loosing a son, and to the delight of musical party hosts who could now hire him openly, Ali shaved his beard, dropped his sacred uniform and donned a Frangi suit, a chapeau, and a tie. Gone were the sad songs of lamentations. His popularity as a new singer of old and new love songs far exceeded his previous reputation. So did his fees, according to the circulating gossip, confirmed by his ownership of a second-hand car.

"Whatever God has ordained, we cannot change." Amirza Hasan was saying as he sat in Mamadali's large living room. "We must surrender to His will and trust His infinite wisdom." He had come to officiate at a memorial service for Saria's older sister, Great Auntie. He was having funeral halvah and tea, talking to the mature men at the gathering, including Mamadali and me. His words were intended to give comfort to the grieving family, but it was obvious that he was also consoling himself about his wayward son. Amirza Hasan had clearly surrendered to God's Will, and that was that. His face was still as kindly and as peaceful as I remembered. He hadn't changed much except for his long beard, now pure white. His short hair, now grey, was showing from underneath his clean white turban. He had a thick warm robe on, to suit the season. He had evidently refused to succumb to modern modes of transportation, at the cost of looking silly even to some of his own colleagues. His mule was parked at the door just as it had been those long years ago. Surely, it couldn't be the mule Mamdali and I had our Thursday rides on? Was it a second or a third mule? Was it still a free source of joy for the children accompanying their mothers to marsia seances? The occasion was too solemn to pose such questions.

GET A CHAPEAU AND A DIPLOMA

HAJ ALI, A CLOSE AND OLD FRIEND OF MY AGED FATHER, was, for a brief period when I was twelve, the perfect model of a grandfather. Inwardly and outwardly, I wanted to be like him when I grew old. (His son, the professor of engineering, who had studied in France, was a candidate for the perfect model of a father, but my mind wasn't quite made up about him yet. For one thing, the unusual profusion of French words in almost every sentence uttered by the professor made his speech incomprehensible to me.) A comfortably-off, retired businessman, Haj Ali was always clean-shaven and clad in an immaculate, well-pressed suit. His shoes, his necktie, and his chapeau seemed to be copied from those of Western movie stars, whose pictures adorned weekly magazines. He talked as if he knew everything worth knowing. He himself decided what was worth knowing, of course, and this very capability of his impressed me immensely. He talked of current world affairs as if he had a hand in their direction, of Churchill and Roosevelt and Stalin as if he had appointed them all, of Truman who was not nearly as competent as the late Roosevelt, of the exiled King of Iran, Reza Shah, who knew exactly how to run the country and how to deal with the old reactionary forces in the society, and of the current Shah, who was still too young and too powerless to do anything of consequence. He knew why the West had prospered while the East stagnated, why we were not yet ready for democracy, why most of our streets were unpaved and dusty right in the middle of the twentieth century, and why we had failed to produce an Albert Einstein or a Charles Lindbergh.

How different Haj Ali was from that other equally close and equally old friend of Father's, Kabl Hasan, the small farm-land owner. The epitome of reaction according to the former, the latter savored not only his village dialect, but also his traditional village clothes, reclaimed from his moth-ridden closets just after the most recent occupation of the northern provinces of Iran by the Russians. This occupation had resulted in the disintegration of the former Shah's regime and the announcement of a new list of dos and don'ts for the confused citizenry. Among other things, the modern Western dress, so abhorred by the traditional men and women, had ceased to be compulsory. This delighted Kabl Hasan no end. The Bolshevik heathens from Russia seemed to be more God-fearing, after all, than the old Shah, who had forced Kabl Hasan to wear those ridiculous foreign garments and hats so unsuitable for saying one's daily prayers in. He could, he said, understand people putting up with government dress rules out of fear, but now that the ban had been lifted, what was the excuse for "some people" who did not return to their godly ways? (He made sure we knew Haj Ali was one of them.) Did some people still have to wear a necktie, which was really a stylized cross originating from the Crusades, and thus an affront to the Right Faith? Did some people still have to shave their beards while they knew full well that it was expressly forbidden according to the most authoritative chroniclers of the lives, deeds, and utterances of the original leaders of the Faith? Did they also have to use this after-shave perfume, this totally unclean alcohol-based fluid, which would render invalid all their daily prayers, assuming that they hadn't, God forbid, stopped praying altogether? Did they have to let their sons join youth groups for the purpose of playing musical instruments? Did their wives and daughters have to bare their heads and faces in the street for every stranger to see?

Of my father's close friends, who dropped in often to chat with him, these two had such diametrically opposite world views, manners, and dress codes, the mere presence of each was so irritating to the other, that they found it absolutely necessary to avoid each other's sight. This was quite unusual, for they were from the same small town, had known each other since childhood, and had perhaps attended the same old-fashioned school for boys. They had certainly fled together, with my folks, from the World War One massacres of their hometown of Salmas.

Almost all those refugees from villages and towns like Salmas who ended up in Tabriz, the big city, stuck to their ilk to ease the pain of exile, even after thirty or forty years. For most of them, starting a new life in Tabriz must have been something akin to immigrating to a new country. They still felt somewhat insecure. They clung to their ancient village traditions; they even kept their own dialect of Azeri Turkish. Older folks were especially close to each other. Most of them took walks together in the city park; they discussed politics while sipping tea and smoking waterpipes in *Salmaslilar,* a teahouse that had gradually acquired the name of their old town. Not these two men. I never saw them talking to each other, but my father said they had tried in the past. Father was, I came to assume, the only friend they shared.

Haj Ali considered himself a true believer in the Faith. Being a man of means, he had even made the dutiful pilgrimage to Mecca, and was thus addressed as "Haj Ali," as opposed to just plain "Ali." He found his own version of religion completely consistent with his modern ways. When he talked of thick-headed incorrigible reactionary men who didn't really know God, no matter how often they said their prayers, I knew he had the other man in mind as a prime example. "A herd of sheep" he called them, "slaves of old habits and meaningless rituals; all form, no content." He also despised a certain other Haj Ali, a very rich man about town, who had a mosque renovated at great expense and financed spectacular passion plays during the mourning months, but was rumored to have shady business practices. "God can do without servants like him," opined our Haj Ali, "all form, no content."

A lot of old men around Haj Ali respected him, even if they didn't like him much. For one thing, they needed him as one of the few men in their circles who "spoke French". When they had telegrams from their relatives or business associates in Istanbul, they would run to Haj Ali for translation. I once asked him when and where he had learned French. "What French? It is Turkish," Haj Ali explained, "and I know the Latin alphabet, which the Turks have switched to, on Ataturk's orders. I simply read the telegrams to them." But he didn't correct the people who came to him for translation. They wouldn't understand the difference, he assured me.

Kabl Hasan couldn't afford, and thus wasn't required, to make the pilgrimage to Mecca. Instead, he had done the next best thing: he had visited the shrines in Iraq, including Karbala, a trip that had entitled him to prefix his given name by "Kabl", a corruption of "Karbala'i". Poorer people than him would have to be satisfied with a visit to the city of Mashad in Iran, which housed a lesser, but more accessible shrine, resulting in the entitlement to a "Mash" before their names. Kabl Hasan had made several pilgrimages to Mashad, but nobody was called "Kabl Mash Mash Hasan or "Haj Kabl Ali." It just didn't work the way "Herr Doctor Doctor" did.

Kabl Hasan was against most of the things I learned in school. Anomalously, and surprisingly to me, he did not think that I should leave school right after elementary grades, before I was indoctrinated by evil ideologies. He had decided, after conversations with me, that I could handle it, and that my faith could withstand it all the way to the end of junior high school. Somebody with a strong faith like me had to learn about heresies out there, and then counter them intelligently. He complimented me by suggesting that after ninth grade I join a seminary. He did not object to my Western-looking attire; he knew that school uniforms were still compulsory, Russian occupation or not. The uniform was temporary anyway, he said, and I could tolerate it until I enrolled, God willing, in his recommended seminary.

I had many conversations with both men, all quite pleasant. Was it diplomacy on my part? Was it that I really found both of them fascinating in their own opposite ways? Was it because I listened much more than I talked, just as a good kid was supposed to do? It is true that I was in awe of Haj Ali, and I wanted to be like him when I grew old, and not like Kabl Hasan or like my father, who was definitely much closer to Kabl Hasan in his cosmology than to Haj Ali, but I had to admire Kabl Hasan for his absolute consistency. He had certain assumptions, almost mathematical axioms, from which all his pronouncements followed simply and logically; there was no way out once you agreed to his axioms. Compared to his, Haj Ali's statements, impressive and forceful as they were, lacked in rigor and consistency. I kept wishing that Haj Ali could formulate his hypotheses and conclusions the way Kabl Hasan did.

Inconsistency was what brought my total admiration for Haj Ali to an abrupt end. It happened while he was relating to me the advice he had given his son the professor twenty years before. The son, having won a Government scholarship to study for an engineering doctorate in France, had hesitated in going, because he felt unprepared for the task. Haj Ali would have none of it. "Go son," he had said, "go! The opportunity may never present itself again; go and do what you want in Paris, but come back with a Chapeau on your head and a diploma in your hand! You have to do this to be respected." He probably had a point. But I told him that circumstances had changed in twenty years. There were many more people wearing *Frangi* hats and clothes now, and a lot of them had diplomas in their hands or on their office walls. I didn't tell him that I hadn't forgotten all those form-and-content pronouncements of his. I didn't tell him that his image as a role model had just collapsed before my eyes. I realized that his practical counsel was being reported for my benefit, because he knew that I dreamed of studying abroad. For a brief moment after this conversation, though, taking Kabl Hasan's advice and enrolling in the local seminary seemed an attractive alternative.

Had the son, the professor, taken Haj Ali's advice to heart, then, and gone a step further, sporting not only Frangi apparel, but also Frangi speech, to be on the safe side? Did he think he was getting more respect by not talking like a normal person? My high school teachers, most of whom dressed as elegantly as the professor did, and one of whom was even as French-educated as the professor was, didn't talk like him. "He doesn't know what he is talking about," said my self-confident and ever-skeptical older brother after a brief encounter with the professor. "I bet," he went on, "that he doesn't even have a real diploma." But how could he be a university professor then? I wondered aloud. As was usual for him, my brother offered a possible explanation for his claim. "Don't you remember," he asked me, " what we read in a weekly magazine recently about the French cartoon fiasco?"

Yes, I remembered. In the late thirties, it seemed, a Paris newspaper had published an uncomplimentary cartoon about the ruling Shah of Iran, at the zenith of his power at the time. The Shah, understandably outraged by the insult, demanded an unconditional apology from the French Government. When the demand was refused, an extra-ordinary pedagogical step was taken by the autocrat, according to the magazine account: among other retaliatory measures, the

Shah ordered all the Government-supported Iranian students to leave France immediately. Many were transferred
to other European schools, but there were some doctoral
students, having fulfilled most of the requirements for the
completion of their degrees, for whom it was difficult to
dislocate. These were among the ones that had, with great
fanfare, been dispatched to European universities several
years earlier. Their mission had been to equip themselves
to the fullest extent with modern scientific and engineering
know-how in order to become better servants to their king
and country. They asked for an extension, said the magazine
article, to get their diplomas. But the wounded and angry
Shah was adamant. "Come back," was his unambiguous di-
rective now, "and your diplomas will be awarded at home."

I had read this, but couldn't quite believe it, because the
magazine specialized in juicy anti-royal-family stuff. "Take
this other professor," suggested my brother, irritated by my
hesitation in believing the story, "the one who wants to be
elected to the parliament now. You know why? Because he
can't teach any longer; his students were too smart for him."
He was talking about a mathematics professor referred to as
"the 17-problem man" by his students. The students claimed
that the man had memorized exactly 17 hard problems and
their solutions, and could do no other problems unless they
were routine. "How are they so sure about 17?" I asked my
brother, when he reminded me of the nick-name. "Over the
years, several generations of students have put together a file
of all his examination problems," he explained, "they used to
fear his difficult finals before. All they have to do to pass the
final now, is to memorize the solutions to the 17 compiled

problems, knowing for sure that their three examination problems would be from the list. They swear the success rate has been one hundred per cent in the last couple of years. Apparently, the man can't fool them any longer; he poses as a learned scholar and talks, walks, drinks, and dances like a Frenchman, but everybody can tell his diploma is fake." This form-and-content matter was getting more complicated by the day. Who was more for form than content now? Haj Ali or Kalb Hasan? You couldn't accuse the former of having no form, and the latter of having no content. You could say about Kabl Hasan, at least, that his form faithfully represented his content.

Kabl Hasan's perfect consistency kept fascinating me until he digressed, one summer afternoon in my father's presence, from his abstract discourse on God, Man, and Nature, and decided to educate me on women. Not coincidentally, I was starting to notice girls at the time. I couldn't believe how disdainful a view Kabl Hasan held of the opposite sex, a view which he said was based on his knowledge of history and the Scripture. Were they anything but an impediment to a young man's pursuit of faith and knowledge? he asked. No, he answered firmly. They were either a trap set by Satan to allure pure men, or an obstacle devised by the Almighty Himself to test the strength of our character. He wasn't quite sure which. But, wait a minute, I thought to myself. How could this beautiful girl whose school route crossed mine every day, and who was, according to a school-mate of mine who knew her brother, already an accomplished violinist, possibly be either a trap or an obstacle? To me, she looked more like an irrefutable proof of God's exquisite taste in sculpture. No, this was it. There was only one possible verdict: consistent or not, I decided, Kabl Hasan was dead wrong.

MY TEACHER'S SCANDALOUS TRANSFORMATION

"I WANT SOMEBODY WITH GOOD, LEGIBLE HAND-WRITING," announced Mr. Haami, the history teacher in my new school. He was addressing us seventh-grade students on the very first day of the school year. I knew I was a candidate, and I wasn't too shy to admit it. But I had a good idea of what was coming next; so I hoped somebody else would volunteer. However, several of my classmates nominated me. Mr. Haami was a former neighbor of mine who had, three years earlier, served as my substitute teacher. This happened in the fourth grade and lasted several weeks, while our regular teacher was on convalescence leave. I was surprised now that he recognized me as soon as he turned his eyes toward the student in the fifth row whose location had been pinpointed by the elevated fingers of my classmates. "Good," said Mr. Haami, "I remember you doing my grade sheets in elementary school. You did a great job." Then he handed me a thick manuscript and asked me if I would be kind enough to copy it for him in my good hand. Sufficient kindness for performing the task was always presumed in such circumstances as this.

The manuscript was Mr. Haami's bachelor's thesis. Like a few other teachers, he had been attending the University of Tabriz at night while he taught school in daytime. This had already resulted in Mr. Haami's promotion to the rank of junior high school teacher. He was on his way to becoming a teacher in the "second cycle," that is, senior high school. This would happen when he got his bachelor's degree, which would mean raised salary and prestige. His thesis, written for a degree in the Faculty of Literature, was mainly, and I thought oddly, concerned with the consequences of British imperialism in Iran. This was 1948, and typewriters had long been in existence, but the old-fashioned professors of the Faculty of Literature detested the look of their beloved Persian words in the admittedly ugly typewritten form. So did my septuagenarian father, who had recognized my talent in early childhood and had me seriously trained in calligraphy, "the noblest of arts," according to him, thereafter using my services for all his formal correspondence.

Mr. Haami, now probably in his late twenties, was wearing a well-tailored suit and tie. He was clean-shaven and fashionably cologne-daubed. His shoes were laced and shiny. His hair was long, well greased, and covered with a shapely chapeau, when out-doors. This represented no less than a total metamorphosis from those days of teaching fourth-grade students. He was evidently less poor now. I remembered his thread-bare pants, which kept developing bigger and more numerous see-through spots until we, the neighborhood kids, were able to tell beyond a shadow of doubt that he was wearing no underwear. He had, according to my mother's reliable sources, had to support not only a mother living with him, but also a step-mother, and three orphaned half-siblings inherited from his late father. By now the brothers and sisters must have become self-supporting,

I concluded from appearances. This only explained his apparent prosperity, but not his modern look and demeanor.

As I walked home that afternoon with the raw exposé of British imperialism under my arm, I couldn't help thinking of the fourth-grade days with Mr. Haami. During that period, he was responsible for teaching us every subject except for physical education, calligraphy, and music. Two hours a week were devoted to each of the first two, and one hour to the third. This left the remaining twenty-one hours for Mr. Haami to share his wisdom with us generously, and to train us to become good citizens. Minimal standards of good citizenship had already been defined by the state, which prescribed uniform syllabi for the various courses. It also assigned approved textbooks. Now Mr. Haami was a sincerely religious man, who attached particular emphasis to matters of faith in all of the courses he taught. If the subject matter didn't automatically involve elements of faith, he found ways of introducing some. Quite a few of the parents approved of his godly ways, but the majority thought of him as "a little odd."

Many school subjects presented problems for Mr. Haami at that time. The health course, for example. The compulsory, state-approved textbook for the subject stated, among other things, that alcohol was a disinfectant. According to Mr. Haami, however, alcohol was impure in any form. Thus he made it clear that as soon after a medical application of alcohol as possible, the affected objects and body areas should be washed in the ritual manner necessary for cleansing them. When one of the students, whose carpenter father built furniture for the school, informed him that alcohol-based varnish had been used on the classroom desks, he instructed us not to touch the desk tops with wet or sweaty hands. When another student dared to quote his father on the acceptability of industrial alcohol, as opposed to drinkable varieties, Mr. Haami got impatient. "Alcohol is alcohol," he snapped, and that was that. The reading hours presented another problem: he wondered which true follower of the Faith would have allowed himself to make those drawings of men and women that were printed in our Persian language text. He cautioned us against the temptation to copy them. "Draw flowers, fruits, trees, and buildings," he counseled us, "but no animal or human images, for if you do, then on the Day of Judgment you'll be challenged by the Creator to provide souls for all the soulless creatures you drew." Of course, we didn't have to ask Mr. Haami what the consequences of a direct confrontation with the Creator would be on that Day of Days.

Almost everything in every school subject seemed to be at least partially problematic, but the greatest problem for the virtuous teacher was posed, as I now vividly remembered, by the subject of music. All music was forbidden according to Mr. Haami's strict interpretation of the Scriptures. He was of course powerless when it came to the requirements of the school system in which he was just a lowly teacher of elementary grades at the time. Fortunately for him, the music class was held during the last hour on Thursday, the noon hour, just before the one-and-half-day weekend started. So he would gather his things together, say goodbye to us, and leave for home every Thursday before the music teacher arrived at 11 a.m. He didn't want to see us engaged in the sinful act of learning music. I remembered how this peaceful procedure was violently disrupted one winter day when, in a hurry to leave, he had forgotten his overcoat and had to come back and fetch it. The music teacher was playing the violin and the students were singing when we spotted an extremely distraught Mr. Haami waiting in the school yard, watching us sinners through the window. He had his index fingers in his ears to block the sound of music. But he must have needed his overcoat very badly. After some minutes' wait and no lull in the wicked noises, he made up his mind. He ran into the classroom, an index finger in each ear, grabbed his coat with one quickly freed hand, placed it on his head to cover his ears, and rushed out as fast as he could.

With these refreshed memories of the substitute fourth-grade teacher, I arrived home. I was anxious to start the transcription task. I was hoping that the manuscript would shed some light on Mr. Haami's incredible personal transformation. How had he come to embrace this *Frangi* appearance, the suit, the hat, the tie, and the cologne, all manifestations of heathens' frivolous lives according to the Mr. Haami I remembered? I opened the thick manuscript as soon as I squatted at my home-made low desk. The first chapter seemed to concern itself with generalities. So I decided to start my copying with the second chapter, which dealt with "superstitious beliefs and behaviors." It seemed that Mr. Haami's definition of the term included many things that he had, not so long ago, considered sacred. "Why is it," he now asked rhetorically, "that right in the middle of the twentieth century, some of us still believe that swallowing mud imported from the vicinity of the tombs of Martyrs of the Faith would cure whatever ails us?" This, I thought, would be total heresy according to Mr. Haami of my elementary school years. "Or," the manuscript went on, "take this shameful practice, on the part of brain-frozen men, of keeping their women covered and uneducated in the name of religion. Who benefits from perpetuating such unreasonable customs?"

There were many similar questions asked before Mr. Haami stated with utmost certainty that there could only be one reason for this irrational state of Iranian minds: British interests. "The British wanted us to stay entangled in our superstitious webs," he wrote, "overwhelmed by our otherworldly preoccupations, so that they could easily steal our this-worldly riches, including our oil." This was hot stuff, I thought. "Take a look at the present state of Persian literature," he lamented, apparently remembering that he was, after all, writing a thesis for the Faculty of Literature, "and you can't ignore the fact that what is being encouraged and pushed on us these days, in verse and in prose, is fatalism." Fatalism had served the British interests in Iran very well, he said. He quoted sources maintaining that many of those nice British scholars who published influential books so full of praise for Iranian poetry were in fact agents of the British Intelligence Service. "Why would any civilized, well-educated man go out of his way to celebrate and promote the irrational and reactionary aspects of our culture, unless he had secret motives?"

Now I had to finish the task of transcription as soon as possible. I didn't want the contents of the book to be seen by my father. Otherwise, I feared, he might change his mind about my new school, God forbid. All schooling after sixth grade was considered by some of Father's friends to be detrimental to children's religious faith, a fact I never allowed myself to forget. My twelve-year-old mind had not yet entertained the possibility that my own faith might be vulnerable. I was certain that all the sacred beliefs that Mr. Haami erroneously attacked in his dissertation could be explained to his total satisfaction if only he had taken the time to seek help from a wise scholar. Take, for instance, this complicated matter of the existence of little demons, those fallen angels, mentioned in the Scriptures, which our teacher was now flatly refuting. It so happened that not too long before Mr. Haami started his course, a number of my new schoolmates and I had casually discussed these mysterious, supernatural beings. "I have seen them with my own eyes," claimed one kid, "many times." This was news to me. My grandmother had always been careful not to spill hot water accidentally on the kitchen floor at night, fearing that it might provoke the ever-present, usually invisible demons to criminal action. But she had admitted, when pressed, that she had never seen them except in her dreams. But this friend was now offering a recipe for meeting an assortment of demons while assuring us that they wouldn't harm us. "Just pull your comforter over your head when you go to bed," he directed us, "and make sure that at least one small light remains on in the room. Don't close your eyes, but stare vigorously at the light through the comforter."

That night, as well as several nights afterwards, I followed the instructions to no avail. I consulted a friend of

Father's, not quite as old as him, nor quite as rigid, whom I considered a trustworthy scholar. "It is stupid to expect a visit from the demon world in the flesh," he said with undeniable authority, "if the Scriptures were to be interpreted correctly." He then explained to me that demons, like all angels of whom they formed the lowest class, were invisible, and so were many other things which we never saw but whose existence had been established nevertheless. "Do you see energy, for example?" he asked, lowering himself to the level of a mere physical scientist, "I am oversimplifying the matter for you now, I know, but let us say angels, including the fallen ones, represent energy." That was good enough for me.

"I wish Mr. Haami had consulted a scholar on the matters touching religion," I said to my classmate Habib with whom I had been discussing Mr. Haami's manuscript in strict confidence. He agreed that many blasphemous passages could have been avoided by doing so, but thought that Mr. Haami's faith was now questionable at best. "I saw him the other day," Habib said, "coming out of Hosep's Bar, where customers drink beer and eat pork sandwiches." What a radical transformation Mr. Haami had gone through! The two of us started to wonder for the first time if it was remotely possible that what had happened to Mr. Haami would some day in the far future happen to either of us. We conceded that Mr. Haami's dissertation contained some reasonable ideas worth thinking about. "Except for the sacrilegious material," Habib said pensively. "Except for the sacrilegious material," I agreed whole-heartedly.

I was relieved that at least during his lectures, Mr. Haami never said anything blasphemous, and restricted the subjects of all his attacks to "certain reactionary tendencies in our society." His discreet digressions from the history syllabus usually concerned the British exploitation of the Iranian oil wealth. For further information, he recommended a book entitled "Our Black Gold." We didn't fully understand or appreciate his figures and arguments, but we preferred them to the descriptions of unending battles led by ancient kings and princes. I didn't discuss the history class with my parents, but Habib talked about it with his father, who then immediately formed and expressed the suspicion that Mr. Haami was a British spy. "That is ridiculous," I said to my classmate, "what could the British Government possibly gain from Mr. Haami bad-mouthing and exposing them?" Habib said he hadn't thought of that and would ask his father.

"My father said we kids underestimate the British," he reported back the next day, "and nobody knows what they are after, anyway. Maybe they just want to find out who their friends and enemies are, what with all this talk starting around the country about putting an end to the British exploitation of the Iranian oil."

After seventh grade I wasn't in any of Mr. Haami's courses, but saw him often. When he wasn't in school, he was demonstrating in the streets or parks for his favorite causes. His very urgent and popular cause was of course nationalization of the oil industry, a goal which would be reached, albeit with unexpected consequences, a few years later. But it turned out that Mr. Haami demanded more than just nationalized oil. He wanted peace for the world and social justice for Iran, among other things. He wrote articles in the local paper, distributed copies of Picasso's famous dove of peace, and invited everybody to participate in peace rallies.

Habib and I, now in tenth grade, were persuaded to go to one of these demonstrations planned for "the young people of Tabriz," in the big park south of the city. Since our parents disapproved of most extra-curricular activities, we swapped hats and jackets in order not to be easily recognized by them or their acquaintances. To be on the safe side, I also borrowed a pair of sunglasses to wear. And we went to the park. There was music, poetry, speeches, and an uncountable number of blue banners depicting beautiful Picasso doves. Mr. Haami gave a passionate rendering of the magnificent Persian ode to peace by the contemporary poet Bahar, "the king of poets." I wondered if Mr. Haami remembered his admonishments to us students in fourth grade about drawing pictures of animate objects. I related the story to my companion. "According to what Mr. Haami taught us then," I said, "Picasso would be answerable to the Creator for all these lifeless birds on the banners that he couldn't give life to." When the finale of the program came as the spectacular, simultaneous release of a hundred live white doves by a group of university students gathered under the banner of "Democratic Youth," Habib raised a philosophical eyebrow and said, "This is perhaps a sign that the Almighty is thinking of forgiving Picasso."

The South-Park peace demonstration, which went without incident, wouldn't soon be forgotten. I dismissed the claim of some elders that the organizers had hidden dark agendas. I remembered those dove-freeing democratic university students fondly. I was impressed that, when they so happily marched out of the park, their ranks included quite a few young women, though far outnumbered by the young men. Was it my imagination or were those boys and girls actually holding hands for a brief minute at the height of the march? I couldn't wait to graduate from the all-boy high school, become part of the coeducational university life, and demand democracy. Perhaps it wasn't too early, I thought, for me to join the Democratic Youth movement now. But the ensuing weeks' incidents gave me reason to pause and reconsider: five or six of those university students, one of them female, were arrested after a march that had turned violent. They were jailed for several days. The female advocate of democracy happened to be the daughter of a well-known cleric. What a scandal for the poor God-fearing family, my parents thought. So did almost every parent in the neighborhood. I thought it prudent to postpone further public demonstrations of my quest for democracy.

Mr. Haami and his university friends, having crossed the line of risking scandal, lengthened what a wise old neighbor called their considerable dream list. Mr. Haami had many new demands now: he wanted the fascist municipal police chief out of Tabriz, he wanted the United States out of Korea, and he wanted Franco out of Spain. Not least of all, he wanted the Shah out of Iran. Most of his demands could not be met immediately; some of them could not be met at all. But his last demand earned him, in that fateful August of 1953, a sojourn to Bandar Abbas, the port city in the south of Iran, reserved for the people with impossible demands. A large number of them were accommodated and re-educated in that remote place, known at the time for having the most inhospitable climate in the country with the most primitive tools of dealing with it. An assortment of traditional and modern techniques were rumored to be employed there to encourage the inmates to review and revise their treasonous thoughts.

By October of that year, the daily papers had started publishing signed statements by those who had finally been persuaded to see the light, and had earned their release from exile as a reward. Mr. Haami must have been slow to learn. His name didn't show up on the list of the publicly repentant until late in the winter. When his statement finally appeared, it was, except for the signature, date, and address, exactly the same form letter as the ones published tens of times a day. Prepared, no doubt, by a semiliterate government functionary, every published letter seemed to include the same grammatical and typographical errors. This day's reformed citizens, like those of the days before, formed a random mixture: young and old, rich and poor, modern and traditional men and women, some known communist sympathizers and some outspoken anticommunists. On this particular day, the names of a low-level cleric and a couple of Christian teachers could be observed. After recounting how the *Tudeh*, the communist Party of Iran, had managed to poison the young mind of the particular signing party one way or another, the individual invariably concluded: "Now that I clearly see the errors of my way, I hereby express my total allegiance to my beloved King and Country, and to my Right

Path of the Ja'fari Sect of Twelvers, the official religion of the country. I also declare my utter and unconditional disgust with the former, now illegal and dissolved, Tudeh Party."

My mother's sources said that Mr. Haami was too ashamed to show his face in Tabriz, he had moved to the Northern Provinces to teach, and was exploring the possibility of going abroad to get an advanced degree. An old neighbor said that Mr. Haami deserved what he got for coming from such a good religious family and changing his godly ways by turning Bolshevik. She remembered how nice Mr. Haami had been as a kid, all the way through young adulthood. "His poor mother!" she exclaimed during an impromptu street gathering of neighbors, "how was she to know what demons would get into his brain when he was admitted into the Teachers Training College? They took a perfectly innocent young man who would never shave his beard like heathens; never take his jacket and hat off in public, no matter how hot it was; never miss a prayer, no matter how busy he was; never as much as look at a female form, even in a picture; never go to a movie; never go near a beer hall; and never fail to respect his elders – yes, and made him into you know what. May God have mercy on us all."

"He wasn't a Bolshevik at all;" a young neighbor submitted respectfully, "in fact, he was a very active member of the Third Force, a movement known for its anti-Stalinist pronouncements." The old woman was unmoved. "I don't care which infidel they are worshiping these days;" she said, "if it isn't Stalin, it is somebody else, what's his name?" She paused. "Tito," contributed a sympathetic listener. The woman's teenage grandson, a recent high-school graduate, who had been listening politely, could no longer contain himself. "Some day this nation will wake up and start to appreciate the likes of Mr. Haami and will erect their statues in the city squares," he predicted. "Shut up and mind your own business," warned the grandmother, "do you want to go to prison again? Have you forgotten what happened last summer, when you went around and defaced the city walls with slogans like 'Death to France'?" There was a moment of silence. "It was 'Death to Franco', not France, Nanna," said the embarrassed grandson. "Whatever;" continued the woman, "if it wasn't for the fact that your father knew the police Chief's servant, you would have stayed in jail for months. Just don't forget that."

I remembered my friend Habib's suspicious father, and was curious to know his current opinion. "Why don't you ask my father yourself?" said Habib, smiling knowingly, when I visited him in the bazaar and put the question to him. "He'll be here soon," he added. A good idea, I thought, and waited for the father who duly arrived together with a few of his cronies.

"Mr. Haami may have been an infidel and a socialist," I said to him, "but you have to admit now, after all he has gone through in jail and exile, that your suspicion was unfounded and that he couldn't have been a British spy." The man took a look at me and I could tell that he was preparing himself to address the village idiot. But his words were polite and fatherly. "On the contrary; I am quite certain now," he said with disarming confidence. "Why was he not executed, as recommended by the prosecutor, and just imprisoned?" he asked, while his companions nodded approvingly, "You are too young now, but when you are as old as I am, you will be able to understand all this. Try not to be fooled by appearances." His loyal friends were very quiet in anticipation of more words of wisdom. "I tell you," the man obliged the captive audience, "the British are the most clever and the most devious race God ever created. They are grooming Mr. Haami now for important future assignments. He will complete his education abroad and wait until the time is ripe for him to serve his masters again. He will come back as a popular leader of an opposition party in some future free elections in Iran. Nobody will suspect him, of course, with his brilliant nationalist and anti-imperialist credentials."

ARTS AND SCIENCES MADE EASY

IDEAS, THE WEEKLY PAPER EDITED AND PRODUCED by four of my schoolmates and me, all in tenth grade, was "published" throughout the school year. Publishing meant placing the single copy of the paper on the wall in the central hall of the school building. Modern photocopying had not been invented yet, and mimeograph machines were beyond our means. So just one copy of each issue was painstakingly constructed, mostly by me, since among the members of the editorial board I had the most legible hand-writing. The paper consisted of just one large sheet, about 60 by 100 centimeters, and was arranged in six to eight columns. It was enclosed in a flat glassed box, a frame really, which was locked to keep the paper clean; fellow-students disagreeing with our editorials were not above defacing it. Once a student tried to do the crossword puzzle right on the wall, before we found the box-and-lock solution.

The paper contained short stories, serialized stories, articles on poetry and science; and the editorial board reserved the right to accept, reject, or alter all solicited and unsolicited articles. I don't remember rejecting anything. My colleagues and I took turns writing the editorials, which followed the fashion of the day adhered to by the Iranian press:

they were as provocative as we could make them. They usually concerned the goings-on in the student extra-curricular clubs, choices of text-books for courses, inadequacies of science labs, and the like. Some of us already had four years of experience in this sort of thing. The name of our paper in sixth and seventh grades had been "Youth", which hardly seemed appropriate now that we deserved more dignity. We first changed it to "New Culture", and then, at the end of ninth grade, decided on the current name, which the editorial Board unanimously found more profound. We had no doubt that our paper was essential to the cerebral growth of our large school community. We took pride, openly for enlightening students, and secretly for challenging the faculty and administration. Our only regret was that all the students and teachers in our school were male, and thus we couldn't play a role in widening the intellectual horizons of the female segment of the population.

Sometime early in this fifth year of "publication" we got overzealous. It happened after the vice principal of the school punished a student, I don't remember for what offence, by slapping him in the face. My brief editorial of the week followed. "A terrible incident has been reported by our correspondent," I said without mentioning the vice principal's name. We were naturally appalled by this, I added, promising an in-depth article in the next issue which would discuss the permanent psychological scars corporal punishment could leave on students. This was a big bluff, and the brief editorial had all but exhausted my supply of big words which could be thrown at the administration.

The bluff worked and the ensuing events guaranteed the editorial board's popularity with the oppressed student body. The school custodian appeared suddenly in the middle of our history lesson and asked the teacher to excuse my colleagues and me for a minute. Then he told us that the vice principal had ordered him to remove the paper from the wall and that he wanted the key to the frame that held the paper. Our opportunity for glory had arrived. We refused to hand over the key in the name of freedom of the press. This resulted in the forceful removal by the custodian of the whole heavy frame, which had been anchored, we thought quite securely, to the wall. The violated wall, proof of our paper's struggle for justice, was, alas, repaired after a day or two.

The editorial board gloated over the "banning" of the paper by the authorities, stopped putting out the paper for a few weeks, and blamed the repressive school atmosphere for this absolutely unnecessary hiatus. We then started a new series of the paper, concerning itself entirely with literary and artistic matters; we had done all we could in the political realm, we figured, at least for the time being.

Our ambitions fed themselves. Preparing articles for this new series inspired us to do something really big. Informing the student public was no longer enough, and we wanted to enlighten the public at large. We would start a series of little books, each with one or two topics in science, literature, art, philosophy, and so on. It would be printed and published just like real books, only small in size and in price, but big in content. It would start with low circulation, which would of course grow to who knows what record-breaking heights.

We were positive we could handle it, but first we had to surmount the financial obstacle: Each of us had an allowance of course, but in my case it didn't amount to much more than pocket money. Two of the members of the editorial board came from much richer families and their allowances were more substantial. Every member pledged his entire allowance for the next three months. We also sold some old and used school books. One member sold his old bicycle. Still, we needed more capital. We decided to offer our schoolmates prepublication prices discounted by twenty percent. Our reputation as defenders of the rights of the downtrodden helped, and we were able to sell about a dozen subscriptions, each for six issues. We estimated that it would take a year or so to have six issues out.

Soon we had written enough material for at least three issues: The first booklet ready to go to press was mainly in biology and medical science entitled "Malignant Tumors". The author, Majid, like many of my classmates, wanted to be a doctor when he grew up. But unlike the others, he meant it, and would eventually become an excellent pediatrician. His booklet, really an article about forty pages long, was a credible compilation of facts found in the books and articles as recent as he or his pharmacist father and uncle could lay their hands on. I prepared an article entitled "The Story of the Sky". It was about outer space, stars, suns, and moons. The choice of the title was suggested by the fact that the words for "story" and "sky" almost rhyme in Persian. Another member of the editorial board, Hussen, prepared an article on aesthetics. Monographs were planned on relativity and psychoanalysis.

As soon as we thought we had enough financial capital to proceed, we contacted a printing house downtown and asked for their best deal indicating that we were willing to do as much of the work as they could possibly trust us with. This was an old family-run press specializing in small jobs, like letters of invitation to weddings or wakes. They had a large press in the corner, but many small, hand-operated machines capable of printing sheets of at most thirty by thirty centimeters in size. To this day I wonder with pleasure why the operators of the press were so cooperative: they let us help with inking and turning these wonderful little machines for a discount in the price of printing our booklet. Perhaps they themselves were frustrated authors and enlighteners of minds? They certainly wanted to see us succeed. The only thing they said we couldn't help with was the actual typesetting. We could come in the summer and learn it, they said, and even get paid for helping.

We decided after some deliberations that Majid's medical-science article would be the first title in the series and that it would be printed initially in five hundred copies. A second printing would be easy with the proceeds of the first in hand. It took the type-setter, an extremely serious but pleasant man, about a week to finish the first draft. He was amazingly fast, but he could attend to our book only when he wasn't busy with more pressing jobs. We watched his quick hands with admiration and listened to the music of the little lead letters coming together and forming words on his slate. We proof-read the typescript to perfection and took intoxicated delight in smelling the printer's ink while we helped produce the first issue of our series. Each time the miniature press turned, another sheet consisting of four pages of the 48-page book was reproduced. Every one of the soon-to-be authors handled the printed sheets lovingly and inhaled the inky air that promised fame and immortality.

After another week the book was printed, four pages at a time, collated, covered, and ready to go. I still have a copy of it. The cover has a lemon-yellow background with the word "Ideas" stylized and prominently displayed on it; this was the general title for the series. In large black, block letters is then printed the title of the current issue: Malignant Tumors.

Each of the editors took a few copies for their desks, and we personally and proudly handed a copy to each of the dozen or so subscribers with profuse acknowledgements and thanks for believing in us. The rest of the copies of Issue #1 of the Ideas Series, more than 450 in all, were quickly dispatched to a small bookstore in the center of the business district of Tabriz. As a distributor for our publications, we would have preferred one of the other two bookstores we frequented for the purpose of buying or exchanging used books, especially the one whose proprietor was an old, enlightened, scholarly, and trustworthy father-figure. But a friend of the editorial board highly recommended this little shop, because of its prime location. We offered the shopkeeper a commission fee of twenty percent on sales and he readily accepted. Then he immediately displayed a copy of our book in his small window. I vividly remember the image of our proud little yellow book alongside an arithmetic manual for school kids and a used copy of André Gide's Fruits of the Earth in translation, which I was thinking of purchasing as soon I could afford it. It was a great moment. We were actual authors now; the sky was the limit.

We had anticipated that the second issue of Ideas should be out of press in two to three months. This, however, was based on the assumption of brisk sales. It became clear after the first month that this estimate was optimistic. After the second month about a dozen sales had been made by our chosen bookseller. We started to wonder why we hadn't thought of the general public's lack of taste for serious reading matter. We hoped that word of mouth would in time awaken our potential audience to the merits of the weighty new series published right in their own city.

Twenty-some transactions took place in the distributing shop involving Issue #1 of Ideas, including deals with a few other bookstores at reduced prices, before the editorial board realized that the general public didn't yet deserve our unselfish attempts at broadening their horizons. Maybe in the far future, when we had more money, we'd try it again. In the meantime we had to face the matter of refund that we owed the subscribers. It took us several weeks to pay our debts in installments. In disappointment and disgust we told the bookseller that he could do whatever he wished with the unsold copies of the book. He could sell the bulk of them as scrap in the city bazaar for all we cared. (The merchants in the bazaar were always ready to give kids enough ice cream money in return for a big bundle of newspapers or useless books which they could use for wrapping and packing purposes.) Then the June examinations arrived and the board of editors tried to bury their sorrows in their books and exam papers.

In the summer following tenth grade, Hussen and I took a long walk through the city one afternoon. We looked like regular school kids in our undistinguished, well-worn school uniforms. It was impossible to guess that we were the erstwhile budding aesthete and astronomer, respectively, whose books lay unpublished and unread because of the public's total lack of appreciation. We had indeed forgotten about our failed attempts almost completely while we enjoyed our summer freedom. We were window shopping when we noticed that a shoe salesman, perched on a chair at the store counter, waiting for customers, was leafing through the unmistakable lemon-yellow-covered Issue #1 of Ideas. A pleasing sight, we both thought as we continued to stroll past the shoe shop. Come to think of it, neither of us had actually seen any member of the citizenry holding an open copy of our book in hand. We felt like authors again. Had the negligent public at last seen the light? Were there perhaps new deals being made at the distributor's? Were other bookstores perhaps placing more orders? Should we check again with the distributor? Why didn't he let us know that sales had picked up? Didn't he owe us some money, in fact? How long had he kept us in the dark? How much longer should we wait before we confronted him? Was he perhaps waiting to present us with a big surprise?

It was impossible to walk away from the happy scene. We decided to stroll back and take another slow, discreet look at this representative of our new-found audience. Our curious glimpse at the contents of the shoe store revealed a whole pile of copies of our book in a corner. Hussen and I knew immediately what had happened. The shameless bookseller!

He had, obviously, taken our distraught pronouncements seriously and allowed himself to sell the books in the bazaar for stuffing shoes. He should have at least had the decency to share the ice cream money with the editorial board.

I feel angry at the bookseller just now, while reporting this, but I remember well, and with astonishment, that at the time we were neither angered nor saddened unduly by the fate of our first book. In fact, we were amused enough to play a mild trick on the shoe seller. We feigned interest in his fancy summer shoes, hoping that he wouldn't decide from appearances that we could hardly afford them. Then we meekly approached him and politely excused ourselves for asking, "What is this book about, sir, if you don't mind the interruption?" He looked up from the book and then down on us know-nothing little boys. Obviously certain that we wouldn't understand any detailed answer about the contents, he uttered only three words that my friend and I would never be able to forget: "It is medical."

"SILENCE! SILENCE, PLEASE, GENTLEMEN! His Excellency may come any minute now," Mr. Shahidi, our junior high school art teacher, repeatedly admonished us. The Federal Minister of Education had arrived from Tehran to inspect the province's instructional facilities. My classmates and I were used to Mr. Shahidi's constant pleadings. He had the noisiest class I ever attended. He kept complaining about it and trying to teach us proper classroom manners, but usually to no avail. He lamented the passing of the good old days, apparently no more than a decade before our time, when students worked harder, behaved better, and really appreciated their teachers. He was forever envious of our stern mathematics teacher whose mere presence in our midst resulted in total silence. This morning was one of the very few times during the year that Mr. Shahidi succeeded in keeping our class relatively noiseless, on account of His Excellency's impending visit.

The Minister and his entourage duly arrived at our school late in the morning and started their inspection. Mr. Shahidi was sure our class would be visited by him. For an entire hour, he kept us waiting and drawing, telling us what a great honor it would be to have this chance. Who knew, he said, maybe the Minister would be impressed enough to give us prizes. "Like the time four years ago," he remembered, "when another minister visited my class and gave every single student a prize; so good everyone in the class was."

The Minister did not come to Mr. Shahidi's class. The principal of the school was wise enough to steer him away from the usually rowdy class. Mr. Shahidi was disappointed, although we did get a ministerial visit during our English class at a later hour. No doubt, the English teacher was judged by the principal to be more presentable. The Minister was especially impressed by my cousin Mahmud, who was in the same class with me. "Take his name," said the Minister to his assistant, broadly smiling at Mahmud. We were all left with the distinct expectation that Mahmud would receive a prize as soon as the Minister left Tabriz for the Capital. For weeks after the memorable day, Mahmud would be asked, and then teased, about the imminent arrival of the prize from the Ministry of Education in Tehran. It would never arrive, and fifty years later, Mahmud would still remember the unfulfilled dream. When informed about the visit, Mr. Shahidi said the previous minister had been more generous in distributing prizes. My older brother laughed when I told him about Mr. Shahidi's amazing former class. He said, "If any minister of education had given prizes to every member of any class in any of the schools in Tabriz, during any of the last twenty years, everybody would have remembered it." My brother, for one, recalled no such thing.

"Maybe next time," Mr. Shahidi said hopefully, when the ministerial inspection team left the school later that day and departed from the province. The art class resumed its noisy but peaceful coexistence with the teacher. A couple of

students in class were good at drawing, and made Mr. Shahidi very happy. He assured them that their drawings would
one day grace the pages of national magazines and newspapers. To the rest of us, he kept saying, "Why can't you gentlemen all be like these two?" No matter how hard I tried, I just
couldn't draw. Mr. Shahidi kept advising me to try harder,
but I don't remember any instructions received from him
except on how to shade with parallel pencil lines. "Anybody
whose handwriting is as good as yours can draw," he said
to me dismissively, and never believed that I was doing my
best. "Silence, please, gentlemen," he would plead periodi-
cally, lifting his head momentarily from the newspaper he
was reading. Some students said he was half-drunk most of
the time, but they had no proof except his constantly red
face and what they called "his drunken accent."

Mr. Shahidi was a great believer in learning by example. "Just go to Bajalanlu's studio downtown and look,
look, and look again." Bajalanlu was a young artist whose
realistic drawings and paintings were very popular in
Tabriz at the time. "I have given this young man a lot of
advice," he said, "but, unlike you gentlemen, he is very appreciative of my efforts, and he thanks me every time I go
to his studio." Most of Mr. Shahidi's other grateful advisees
and former students seemed to be out of town for the time
being, and not immediately available for emulation by us
current students. "A lot of them are gainfully employed
by the national press in the Capital," he told us, "some are
teaching at the University of Tehran, and quite a few are in
Rome and Paris, pursuing their studies and holding public
exhibitions of their own recent works." They never forgot

to send him annual greeting cards at the *Nowruz* season, he told us, from wherever they were, and never failed to reconfirm their indebtedness to their former teacher.

Mr. Shahidi was older than all our teachers except for the calligraphy teacher, the famed Taher Khoshnevis, whose very last name meant "one who writes beautifully," and who was my parents' preferred role model for me. My father had high hopes for my becoming the future Khoshnevis of Tabriz, but did not encourage, nor did he even recognize, many other art forms. To be fair, he did not object to my drawing of flowers, birds, or even human forms, which was remarkable. Some fathers whose observance of religious rules seemed no more strict than his were less tolerant in this regard. They believed it sinful to draw an animal in any form. My drawings were okay with Father so long as they were not directly visible by the grownups when they said their daily prayers. This meant, since the praying direction in Tabriz was almost exactly southward, that I could safely place any drawings or pictures on the north wall of the large family room.

Our teacher's ripe age and experience had prepared him well for potentially embarrassing and possibly dangerous confrontations with strict and literal followers of the rules of piety. Everybody knew that when our teacher was in elementary school in Tabriz, a very long time before us, modern schools were almost underground establishments. Their pupils and teachers had been attacked by religious zealots who objected to "French language and Darwinism being taught in schools." Actually, it wasn't until later in high school that Darwin's theory was discussed and foreign languages were introduced. Mr. Shahidi must have been a courageous little boy at that time, not only daring to go to a modern school, but even showing interest in forbidden art forms.

Our teacher must have faced further obstacles as he continued his education during the first decades of the century, which now seemed so ancient to us students. But he had not neglected to gather ammunition for his future battles: he had learned the nuances of religious dicta. This became apparent one day in class, when a student mentioned his pious father's objection to drawing pictures of living things. "But don't forget, gentlemen," he said, addressing the whole class with obvious authority, "that the religious objection applies only to a whole and perfect depiction." Then he clarified the matter to the satisfaction of most of us: "If the human forms you gentlemen draw happen to miss just a tiny, even invisible, part somewhere, as we all know they always do, then they are imperfect and thus exempt." Now it was easy for me to guess why Father didn't object to my drawings at all; they were so clumsy that anybody who took a glance at them would know immediately that they were exempt.

It was known to the students that Mr. Shahidi had a large family, including eight children – a financial burden that a junior high school teacher's salary could not easily bear. Mr. Shahidi had tried extra tutoring, but there wasn't a large market for tutoring in drawing or painting. When he was just a student, Mr. Shahidi had earned added income for the family by helping his father, an illiterate but talented artist whose occupation it was to paint ceilings and walls of fancy houses in Tabriz. This type of painting, many examples of which still existed in my student days, would become rarities in the space of a few decades. They consisted mostly of geometric friezes, some quite intricate. The social, financial, and ideological standing of the master of the household permitting, these ornaments would include original "miniatures," that is, paintings of two-dimensional men, women, flowers, trees, deer, horses, and other creatures in striking colors, ostensibly depicting classical tales of love and war. Sometimes, the wall and ceiling figures were harmonized with those on an elaborate Persian carpet adorning the floor of a rich guest room. Religious families stuck to geometric decorations, which were also more intriguing to me; the miniatures I found generally boring as I grew older. One exception was the guest room of a wealthy and modern relative, whose walls had been done in minute detail by our teacher's father, possibly with help from his young son. As a kid, I had taken great delight, every time I accompanied my mother on a visit to this house, in walking counterclockwise around the huge room and attempting to discern the story from the numerous painted panels. "But how do you say your daily prayers in this room with all these paintings?" I had once asked the hostess innocently. "We have another room with plain walls, dear," the woman had replied diplomatically.

By my student days, Tabriz home-owners no longer seemed to require, or care for, these made-to-order friezes on the walls of their rooms. Besides, it would be beneath Mr. Shahidi's standing in the Tabriz society, as a graduate of the Teachers Training College, and a teacher of high schools, to engage in such a menial job as wall painting. Thus he was resigned to the role of struggling but dignified teacher. Not only were his well-worn suit and white shirt always freshly pressed, and his blue tie neatly tied; he never forgot his matching "pocket square," the small handkerchief folded into a triangle and partially tucked into his breast pocket next to his shiny gilded fountain pen. He owned two *chapeaux;* a white straw one for the summer and a brown velvet one for the winter. He wore a permanent sad half-smile. He never gave a student a bad mark.

The students decided one day to surprise Mr. Shahidi by staying absolutely silent during his class. A classmate had heard from his father that Mr. Shahidi could really teach if he had truly serious and obedient students. Let us see how he can teach, we said. We started the hour with exemplary behaviour, but this didn't seem to strike Mr. Shahidi as curious. He did leave his newspaper aside, though, and started to tell us stories. Not surprisingly, the moral of every tale he told was that we the gentlemen of this class did not adequately value his efforts. But the accounts were interesting. "I used to be a professor of music at the University of Mazandaran..." began his main story of the day, in such a genuinely tragic tone accompanied by such a deep sigh that everybody was immediately sympathetic and respectfully attentive. "Very appreciative students...those young men at the University of Mazandaran;" he reminisced, "so good and so attentive...and so thankful to me forever," he said, "and such a pretty province, gentlemen, such lovely surroundings, and such nice people." Then he erupted into a loud and fierce recitation of the Persian epic poet Ferdowsi's majestic couplets in admiration of Mazandaran's natural glory. "He is drunk again," whispered my bench-mate, "look at that red face!"

Just as I started to fear that he would collapse from over-exertion, Mr. Shahidi stopped yelling and continued with his story of how happy he was in Mazandaran, how he would give half his life to be there again and teach those hard-working and grateful students of the University of Mazandaran. "But don't ever underestimate kismet, gentlemen!" he exhorted us, "Obviously, another destiny had been written for me." Then, as suddenly as it had come, the excitement was gone. "Unfortunately," he said in a very soft voice, "for family reasons, I had to come back to Tabriz." And he sat down, grabbed his newspaper, and motioned us gentlemen to carry on.

Now many students knew that Mr. Shahidi played the *taar*, a popular string instrument. In fact, I had once seen him carrying a taar under his arm. But we had no idea of his music professorship. A few of us were aware that there was no such university. At the time, there were only two universities in the whole country, as far as we knew: the old one in the capital city, and the newly established one in Tabriz. This was confirmed later by asking some grownups in the know, including my older brother. But nobody was about to embarrass Mr. Shahidi with such trivial details. "Maybe he was a music teacher in the high schools of Mazandaran," I said to my classmates. "But high schools don't have music in their curricula," another student reminded me. We did not pursue our speculations any further.

Mr. Shahidi gave us all good marks for mid-year tests and went on reading his newspaper and advising us gentlemen to work harder and learn by example. But he seemed to be ever more given to melancholy. "His creditors," diagnosed one student whose father, it seemed, knew the tight financial situation the teacher was in. The recent weddings of two of his several daughters couldn't have helped, he quoted his father as saying. But appearances never changed. Mr. Shahidi's well-worn suit was still perpetually pressed, his shirt was still white and freshly laundered, his blue tie and handkerchief properly in place. "It is the University of Mazandaran professors' uniform," a few of us joked cruelly but privately. Mr. Shahidi's dignity refused to be affected by his troubles, whatever they were.

The end of the school year was approaching. While our teacher was reading his newspaper one afternoon and we were carrying on, drawing a little and talking a lot, the school custodian knocked on the door and solemnly notified Mr. Shahidi that there were three men in the school yard who insisted on speaking to him right away. The teacher left with the custodian, and through the windows we could see him approaching his callers. We couldn't hear anything, but the men looked so menacing, and our teacher grew so ashen in the face once they started talking to him, that some of us could surmise what the mission was: the men could only be impatient creditors or their collection agents.

I myself had seen men like those three recently, maybe even the very same men, at the door of a neighbor, whose business was rumored to be failing. I remembered my humiliated neighbor and his family members who were now no longer even comfortable saying hello to their old friends. Some neighbors said that it was simply a misfortune, but there were those who thought the man's business failure was a divine punishment for some wrong-doing temporarily unknown to us mortals.

Now sitting in the suddenly quiet classroom, with every student watching our teacher through the large windows, I dreaded poor Mr. Shahidi's imminent ruin in front of our own eyes. His back was toward us, but his shoulders, head, and hands were engaged in the kind of motion that could only be associated with desperate pleading. Whatever promise the teacher was making to them apparently worked. The men left the school yard. Then we watched our teacher slowly turn back and walk toward the classroom. It was a terrifying experience. The class was in total silence when Mr. Shahidi finally entered the room, all composure and dignity. "Gentlemen," he began addressing the class in his habitually soft voice, "remember what I told you about my years at the University of Mazandaran?" All mouths opened and all heads remained still in anticipation. "What did I tell you about those appreciative students? Well, gentlemen, these men you just saw were former music students of mine from the University of Mazandaran. They were here, after all these years, to thank me once again for all I did for them."

CREAM PUFFS AND A BLUE SUIT

TABRIZ, IRAN; SUMMER OF 1950

NINTH GRADE EXAMINATIONS ARE OVER. So is graduation from junior high school, an event of significance in a school kid's life. My schoolmate Hussen and I plan to make some money by tutoring in the summer. There are certain things such as light-weight summer suits and cool shoes that we would love to have, which our meager home allowances can't buy. There is also this little café near our high school that serves heavenly cream puffs and delicious carbonated lemonade; we go there as frequently as we can afford it, which is once every other week. Wouldn't it be nice to go there every summer afternoon, we ask each other in titillating expectation.

We need a suitable place and we need to advertise our services. We solve both problems by approaching an old relative of mine who runs a small private elementary school in the heart of the old city. Since the school is essentially idle in the summer, we propose a mutually profitable deal to him: he would pay for advertising and let us use his classrooms in return for fifty percent of all the fees collected. He accepts without hesitation and we draft an ad. "Good News to All

Students of First Through Ninth Grades Who Have to Take Supplementary Exams in September!" reads the ad in extra-large print on bright orange paper. It promises "Affordable Tutoring! All Subjects Taught!" and offers the amazing rate of one *tuman* per hour. This is indeed cheap; the going rate is much higher; our teachers themselves, who are always in need of supplementing their insubstantial salaries, charge three to four tumans per hour for private tutoring, a fee which only the richer students can pay.

An assortment of students show up to give us a try. A week after the ad appears, Hussen and I have already worked ten or twelve hours each, teaching arithmetic, physics, and "language". A foreign language, which almost always means English, is a required subject, simply referred to as "the language." We can hardly speak English, but this never seemed to stop most of the English teachers in our city school system. What is really required is the kindergarten variety of reading and grammar, and we are confident we can handle it. It so happens that our own secondary school is lucky enough to have one of the few competent English teachers in town. This has led us to believe that we could teach anything an average English instructor could.

We are very excited; this is only the beginning and we can already count on five or six tumans. No money has changed hands yet; we will receive the full fee owed by each student at the end of that student's stay with us – in a clean envelope. We are aware of this long-standing tradition which, I have always assumed, has to do with the respect that scholars and teachers in Iran have claimed to deserve since antiquity. A teacher's efforts on behalf of a student are too noble to be measured in money. One places the money in the envelope to hide the supposed embarrassment that an attempt at this ignoble measurement entails. When the time comes, I will put the envelope in my pocket discretely, utter a subdued word of thanks, and never examine the contents in the payer's presence.

Early in the second week, a boy of about fifteen or sixteen, Rasool, comes to us. He has heard good things about our tutoring methods, he says, and he wants to be tutored on all the "important" subjects of seventh through ninth grades. It turns out that he has a relatively rich but old-fashioned father, one who considers modern education past elementary school, namely after sixth grade, detrimental to a boy's religious faith. (A girl's faith, being of a more delicate fabric, couldn't even stand subjection to first-grade pressures.) His father made him quit school three years ago, Rasool says, and he is now helping his father in the office, and learning to be a junior partner. But he has succeeded in persuading his father, he says, to allow him to take the "miscellaneous examinations" for junior high school.

Meant as a fair chance for people who, for some reason, were not able to attend regular school, these special examinations are offered every year, and a variety of people, young and old, take them. They are not particularly easy, but they concentrate on those subjects which the Federal Ministry of Education has deemed essential. Thus a smart student who has studied only those subjects and is properly coached could pass the entire examination for the junior high school diploma. Coaching is what Rasool wants me to do; he asks me to stop taking new students for the rest of the summer and devote to him as much time as possible. This is pure good luck, I think to myself. I readily agree to the deal and start to teach him all those important subjects in preparation for the September Miscellaneous.

I calculate that with five tutorial hours a day, six days a week, his fees would come to more than 200 tumans, half of which would be mine by late August. This is big money indeed. A hundred tumans is a third of a school teacher's monthly pay; more important, it is forty times my weekly allowance from home. I start to window shop for the summer attire that I would own come September. Credit cards have not yet been heard of, even for adults, so I don't make any purchases, of course. But I come as close as I can. I know exactly what material, and how much of it, I would buy for my suit and how much it would cost me. I picture myself in this shiny blue suit made of genuine British wool – not those cheap Japanese imitations. There are no new ready-made suits sold in the Tabriz bazaar, and I, like everybody else, will have the suit made by a tailor. My richer classmates have their summer suits made by a fashionable Armenian tailor, Andranik, whose services I now book vaguely for late August. He is quite expensive, but my precise calculations allow for his fees, the cost of the material, and even the price of a spiffy pair of shoes I have spotted in a fancy downtown shop.

After the second week, some students have already learned as much as they thought was necessary, paid their dues, and left. So Hussen and I start to reward ourselves. Every day after classes, we take the long walk from the old city to the modern boulevard, where our favorite café is located.

We can be seen there at five o'clock, devouring cream puffs, sipping lemonade, looking at newspapers, and discussing philosophy. On the way home, I digress every day to pass by "Andranik's Tailoring Salon" to enjoy the breath-taking view of the finished and half-finished suits he has been working on, which he proudly displays in his salon's wide windows.

The school whose facilities we are using has to be cleaned and scrubbed for the return of its regular students, and everybody is informed that the last Thursday of August would be the last day of tutorials. Rasool outlasts all our summer students, as expected. On the Wednesday of that last week, he comes to school with old copies of the previous year's miscellaneous exams, which he wants to work out with me, and he says he will bring more the next day. Thursday will be algebra review day.

TABRIZ, IRAN; LAST THURSDAY OF AUGUST, 1950

Rasool does not show up on Thursday morning. Hussen isn't in school that day, but the principal and I wait until noon, sipping tea in anticipation of the discreet envelope containing our fees. It is substantial money that we are waiting for, even by the principal's grown-up standards – about one hundred tumans for each of us. The net monthly income of this little school could hardly be more than 500 tumans during the academic year, and scarcely more than nil in the summer. This gentle, shy, and very polite and proper man must also have plans for spending the extra money. By noon, closing time for the weekend and for the summer tutorials, it is clear that Rasool isn't coming. By the end of the following week, it is also clear that he isn't paying. I will try hard, in the future, to find the reason why we, the principal and I, didn't appeal to Rasool's well-off father in the bazaar. For now, I am too inexperienced in this business, but why isn't the principal suggesting anything? Why am I not asking him for suggestions? Perhaps we entertain no hopes of redress. We know, of course, what the father thinks of modern schools anyway. He would be shocked, no doubt, to find that any service rendered by us half-heathens is worth such an exorbitant remuneration.

My blue suit, so well conceived, is not to be born. All I can do now to get back at Rasool, and I will do it far into the future, is tell the story whenever an occasion presents itself, that is, whenever I meet anybody who knows him.

SHIRAZ, IRAN; SOMETIME IN THE LATE 1960S

I have almost forgotten about Rasool. I am now a professor in Shiraz. At a student gathering, I overhear a familiar name: they are talking about Rasool, who has just returned from his successful studies abroad and is teaching at another university. Vivid memories of being cheated, being deprived of my beautiful blue suit and fancy shoes in that summer of 1950 surface immediately. I may have forgotten Rasool, but forgiving him is clearly still beyond my capabilities. I tell the students what a rascal Rasool was as a young man. A long discussion ensues on the possibility that he is a changed man now, and on whether people can really change that much. I surprise and embarrass myself by how angry I still am after so many years. Then I share my story with a few more people and decide to forget it again.

NORTH-WESTERN IRAN, SUMMER VACATION OF 1971 OR 1972

A group of my friends and I are taking a walk in the park. Strolling in the opposite direction are Rasool and a couple of other people. Rasool and I recognize each other instantly. His face turns ashen, he leaves his companions and asks me if he could have a private word with me. He is obviously aware that I haven't done a good job of keeping our little secret to myself. Is he going to apologize now, after more than twenty years? If he does, would I forgive him? He is in a hurry to rejoin his waiting companions, so he doesn't waste any time. "How much?" he asks me point-blank. "How much money do you want to shut up?" he clarifies himself after a short, angry pause. I am at a loss for a reply. I am trying very hard not to show my anger. "Not a single penny," I manage to say, still feeling haunted by the ghost of the unborn blue suit. "Not a single penny, not a single penny" I catch myself repeating, "because even your yearly salary wouldn't be enough now." But then I gather myself together and mumble a promise not to talk about the incident to anybody who knows him.

HALIFAX, CANADA, SUMMER OF 1997

I am having lunch in Halifax with an old school friend from Tabriz and now, by my good luck, a Dalhousie University colleague, who has just returned from an overseas conference. He is anxious to tell me about this nice guy he met at the conference whose name and title I immediately recognize as Rasool's. My friend's report of the meeting disarms me forever: Rasool asked him, he says, during their coffee-break small talk, whether there were other fellow-Tabrizis living in Halifax. Upon stumbling on my name, Rasool was "elated" and dispatched my friend to bring me special, heart-felt gratitude and greetings. "You can't imagine just how indebted I am to this guy Radjavi, your friend;" Rasool said to him, "I wouldn't be near where I am today without his selfless efforts. He taught me everything I had to know in junior high school, tutored me in every subject necessary for getting my diploma, and – you won't believe this – he refused to accept even a single penny in return."

MY SINGLE DAY IN MILITARY SERVICE

"REPORT FOR INSTRUCTIONS PROMPTLY at 4:30 a.m. on Saturday" said the corporal in charge of registration for the military draft lottery. He was addressing me and Parviz, my friend and neighbor. I was applying to participate in the lottery, but Parviz had already registered as a volunteer for military service. The Imperial Army had decided that year, as in the past few years, that the supply of "diplomates," meaning high school graduates, was greater than needed for active duty. As far as His Majesty's Armed Forces were concerned, all the male Homo sapiens were divided into exactly two convenient, non-overlapping categories: diplomates and non-diplomates. You were in the first category, for instance, if you had a doctorate in physics from Sorbonne or Princeton, and in the second if you couldn't write your name. There was no lottery for the non-diplomates; they were all needed and wanted. They cost the Army very little to draft and keep occupied. They were also very useful: a great many spent their two service years as orderlies for officers. This often meant that they were placed in a high-ranking officer's household as man-servants for scarcely more compensation than room and board. Diplomates, on the other hand, got far better treatment when drafted; they started as students of the Officers Training College, then became "duty officers," were paid respectable salaries, and never served as orderlies.

Parviz and I, both twenty-one years old, had different reasons for being at the registry, although we were both diplomates. He wanted to make sure that he was being treated as a volunteer and that his name was not accidentally put on the lottery list. He didn't have a job and hadn't finished college. He didn't like chemistry, the field of study assigned to him according to his ranking in the university entrance examinations. He lived at home, supported by a rich and influential father, Haj Rahim, who expected him to do well in college. Parviz was fed up with his father's strict household rules and regulations. He desperately wanted to get out of that house. "At any price," he kept saying. In the preceding years there had been fewer volunteers than His majesty's Army wanted, and it was predicted by potential draftees that the number of volunteers on this round would be at least 500 out of the total of about 5000 young eligible men who had registered this September. The Army needed 1000 young diplomates. I was relying very heavily on my good chances, better than eight in nine if the rumored estimates were to be believed, that I would be exempted from peacetime service as a result of the lottery.

I had just graduated from college, and there was nothing in the world that I wanted to do more than studying for a higher degree in mathematics. If I could continue my education without interruption, my compulsory military service could have been deferred. But, at the time, no Iranian university offered a graduate program in mathematics. To obtain a study exemption I would have to go abroad, which I couldn't afford except with government support. A scholarship was being promised to me by the Ministry of Education, but not yet sufficiently firmly to satisfy the military arm of His Majesty's Government. As it turned out, it would take more than a year for the promise to be fulfilled. Thus I had no choice in reporting for the September lottery, but dreaded the possibility of being drafted, which would mean losing the scholarship if it ever materialized.

I was the only one who knew that Parviz had volunteered. He had told everybody else that he was applying for the lottery just as I was, because "a chance like this might never again present itself." Haj Rahim would be furious if he knew the truth. The father wanted Parviz to stay out of the Army for as long as possible. Haj Rahim had an excessive fear of the damage peer pressure in the Army would do to young Parviz's moral fiber. I found this baffling, because he had already sent his older son to Paris to study medicine. Surely, most parents thought, Paris life would be more damaging to the average moral fiber than army life. Parviz begged his father to send him to Paris too, and defer the military service in the process. No, said the father, and reminded Parviz that his older brother had not passed the entrance examinations for college, and was thus subject to immediate drafting. "That is my father's logic," Parviz complained to me, "I am smarter than my brother, at least I pass one entrance examination, but get to stay home with him; my brother fails them all, and gets sent to Paris!"

With substantial persistence on the part of Parviz, and with a little deceitful help from me, Haj Rahim had consented to the purported registration for the lottery. By passing the entrance examinations three years earlier and having a choice in my field of study, I had gained immense respect in Haj Rahim's eyes. It was true that he couldn't see why any young man in his right mind would choose mathematics over civil engineering, for the latter field promised a very lucrative future at the time. But he made allowances for this eccentricity in my case when I told him that I planned to win a scholarship to go abroad, get a doctorate, and become a university professor eventually. He started referring to me as "the professor" right away, more to punish his sons than to please me. "You'll never amount to anything," he once admonished Parviz and his younger brother in my presence, "unless you start working as hard as the professor here." The contrast seemed to enrage him. "Take a look at the professor," he continued, "and look at yourselves." A torrent of questions and answers then followed. "Did the professor have all the comforts of life that I provided for you? No. Did he ride to school in a chauffeur-driven, private family car? No. Did he have a swimming pool at home? No. Did his parents have a servant or a maid to free him from household chores? No." Haj Rahim was on a roll. How violently should I protest, I asked myself, if he went on with "Did the professor have enough to eat at home before he left for school every day?" Fortunately, he stopped asking questions and hurried to the concluding remarks. "Yet he did a hundred times better in school than you idiots," he said, wrapping it up, "I shouldn't have made all those sacrifices for you undeserving brats."

So it was with considerable confidence now, after my graduation, that Haj Rahim turned to me for consultation on this important matter. "Professor," he addressed me just before the draft registration date, "you are the expert in mathematics and statistics; is it really true, as Parviz claims, that there is an excellent chance this year of being exempted from peacetime service for good?" I knew he couldn't trust Parviz. "Yes, of course" I replied authoritatively, giving a technically truthful answer.

To report at the appointed time at the out-of-town barracks, Parviz and I had to get up at 2:30 that Saturday morning. An hour later, we took one of the special buses sent to collect the eligible diplomates from all over Tehran. It was an overcrowded bus, filled mostly with total strangers. But everyone seemed to be in an unusually jovial mood. We sang and we joked around. The lottery hopefuls teased the volunteers about the small taste of army life they were getting on the bus. Our jam-packed bus finally arrived at the barracks shortly after four o'clock, almost simultaneously with more than eighty other such buses, all bursting with qualified male diplomates. The roads immediately leading to the huge drill field surrounded by the barracks were not paved; neither was the field itself. It hadn't rained in Tehran for several hot months, and the dirt on the the ground had turned to soft dry powder. The buses created such a dust storm that we couldn't see anything or anybody as we disembarked. We heard one passenger singing familiar couplets from Ferdowsi's epic Book of Kings. They came from an ode to the brave warriors of ancient Iran, whose formidable horses were capable of altering the mythological layers, seven each, of the

sky and earth: "When the horses had traversed that vast the-
atre/ Only six layers of the earth remained/ But the sky had
now gained an eighth/... ." We treated the singer to thunder-
ous applause.

When the dust had settled enough for us to regain the
use of our eyes, a water-spraying truck arrived and started to
fight the dust. "You are late," said a bus driver. "You are early,"
countered the dust fighter. Everybody clapped and cheered
for one last time, before a loud whistle informed us that it
was now 4:30 and the official day was starting. "Quiet!" announced the loudspeakers, "Follow the instructions carefully." We were divided into small groups each of which was
assigned a sergeant, who proved to have complete control
over our movements for the next twelve hours on that hot,
dry September day. The loudspeakers spoke once more and
said that "the statistics of registration" were being studied,
and we would be notified of the results "in due course."

That was it. We wouldn't hear from the loudspeakers again for many hours. In the meantime, each of our
sergeants-in-charge would order his group to march a few
hundred meters, to the tune of his whistle, and be stationed
on a different spot. This happened every hour or so, and the
destination was invariably sunnier and hotter than the original location. "This is the Army;" whispered my comrade in
marching, "the illiterate sergeants want to get even with all
of us diplomates." "Why can't we stand in the shade?" asked
another diplomate. "You don't ask questions in the Army,"
replied the first. Our sergeant, who seemed to be quite good-
natured, overheard the last exchange, smiled and agreed.
"Besides," he allowed, "as you see, there isn't enough shade

for all the groups as noon approaches." I was touched by the egalitarianism of it all.

Hot noon arrived. Everybody was sunburnt, thirsty, and hungry. Water was provided, but no food. Some of us had brought sandwiches, and all of us, including our sergeants had assumed that we would be done by noon. But there was still no official news from the loudspeakers. Fresh sergeants arrived and took charge as the morning sergeants promptly left, presumably for lunch. Our replacement commandant seemed to be new at this, and took his job more seriously than the preceding one. Parviz had been separated from me by the morning's random groupings, but there was another volunteer standing next to me. He was getting more irritable by the minute, cursing himself for knowingly getting into "a life situation like this for the next two years."

"What is taking so long?" we were asking each other continually. All our sergeant would say was "a committee is conducting the lottery upstairs, but the outcome could only be finalized by His Majesty's orders." Apparently, for some reason, there was a delay in reaching His Majesty for a signature. Once in a while, a general or a colonel would walk by, on his way from one building to another, and we were all ordered to stand at attention mimicking our leading sergeants.

We weren't allowed to leave our group's sunny location, but we were permitted to mingle a bit and speak to the other members of the group, so long as we didn't disturb our formation (arranged by height of course) too noticeably. Various conjectures started to be generated and circulated. Outrageous, second-hand army stories were told. "Maybe they decided to take us all this time," said a comrade to me, "maybe a war is being planned; you can say good-bye to your plans for studying in America." In that summer of 1956 it was hard to imagine Iran at war with any nation. "A more realistic possibility exists;" I offered, "there are more diplomates in the country now, as we all know. This means that there are fewer non-diplomates to go around as orderlies for officers. This emergency may necessitate using diplomates as orderlies." I meant this as a pure joke, but my comrades' mood had already grown too pessimistic to find it funny.

A particularly talkative comrade wasn't so sure that life was as bad for non-diplomate draftees as we were led to believe, after all. "Why my own cousin couldn't pass his final high school exams," he said, "and was drafted just about this time last year, and sent to a border post as an orderly for a very nice colonel. Would you believe that the colonel's beautiful daughter wasted no time falling in love with my cousin?"

I contemplated once more the undesirable possibility of being drafted. "It won't kill me," I comforted myself, "I could read during my spare time; I could take along my newly acquired book on measure theory." Then I remembered how, as a very young boy, I had admired the military uniform, and especially the knee-high boots, worn by my older cousin, the Lieutenant. The spectacle of the lieutenant sitting on his fancy chair with the kind of dignity which only a military uniform could lend a man in my young eyes would have been memorable enough. But there was more to this awe-inspiring picture. His orderly, who of course kept the black leather boots shiny at all times, would be summoned to help my cousin put them on or take them off. It looked like a truly hard job to handle those awkward boots, and some officers kept handy a special device for the purpose. "Good thing my cousin has an orderly," I thought, "otherwise his mother would have to remove his boots for him."

It was hard now to remember exactly at what age the military uniform had lost its immense glamour for me. I awakened myself from my reminiscences, growing more impatient to know the lottery results. It was only a few days earlier that I had been warned by one of my eminent professors to postpone two things as long as it was humanly possible, in order to continue my studies successfully: getting married and getting drafted.

His Majesty must have become available for signing the decree around three in the afternoon. There was a lot of activity in one of the buildings for an hour or so, keeping us very nervous. Around four o'clock, the loud-speakers came to life. "By the orders of His Majesty, the Commander-in-Chief, there will be no lottery this time," started the presiding officer, shocking us lottery hopefuls. "There were 1013 volunteers for this round," he continued, "and, as you know, the Imperial Army needed only 1000 diplomates this time. In order to respect the patriotic sentiments of those who have volunteered to serve his majesty, we welcome them all. Congratulations!" A few tense moments of silence followed before the good news came for the rest of us: "Those of you who registered for the lottery should report to the Registry in the city center next week to get their permanent peacetime exemption cards." Deafening applause and whistling was heard from every direction. I was overwhelmed by my good luck; my military service was completed in one day.

Receiving this news, combined with my innate optimism, was tantamount to getting a passport for studying abroad.

The groups were dispersed and we were ordered to find our morning buses and bus-mates. It took us a substantial amount of time to do so, but nobody seemed to mind. Everybody was happy, I thought, until I found Parviz, who was in a dark, inconsolable mood. His original plan, of simply letting Haj Rahim believe that he got unlucky in the lottery, had to be revised now. He was scared of being found out, eventually, by "*Haj Agha.*" This was his way of referring to his "master" in a show of mock respect. We each had a sandwich and a drink at our favorite café, where we discussed the situation for a couple of hours before going home. He finally decided to pretend that he was the victim of a mistake on the part of the semiliterate corporals handling the registrations before the lottery day. Fortunately for Parviz, his last name was a common one, probably shared by more than a few other diplomates in each round. "Besides," he assured himself and me, "Haj Agha will never doubt the professor." He didn't want me to lie too much, he said; I should just not contradict him when he told his father that we had registered for the lottery together.

When we arrived at his home after sunset, we had hoped for gradually breaking the suitably edited news to the master. But Haj Rahim was waiting for Parviz at the door, and he seemed ready to kill. "May your head be covered by ashes, and mine too, for the kind of son I have brought up," he yelled uncontrollably, ignoring me. "My God! What did I do wrong?" was only the start of his familiar bombardment of Parviz by rhetorical questions. Mercifully, he kept the professor out of it. Parviz's mother managed, between Haj Rahim's shouts, to inform me and Parviz that the happy news of the induction of all the 1013 patriotic volunteers to His Majesty's active service had already been announced on the radio during the early evening report. She also whispered to Parviz that another neighbor had already told Haj Rahim that "Parviz got in." The master's spies must have been hard at work while Parviz and I had our strategy meeting at the café.

"An error, a stupid error, was committed by the illiterate clerks," Parviz kept repeating. When Haj Rahim was finally able to hear Parviz's voice over his own, he surprised me by believing his son unconditionally: surely, it must have been an error; no son of Haj Rahim's, no matter how ungrateful and how immature, would be stupid enough to leave the luxury of such a home for the misery of the Army life.

Haj Rahim started immediately to rectify the error by using his "influence on a highly placed Army general" he knew. He called the friendly general, who promised to look into it as soon as possible. He did report back the next day: "It is possible, but not very likely, that an error has been committed, but once signed by His Majesty, an order to induct cannot be reversed, except perhaps by God Himself; I am sorry." The implication was that not even the general was God enough in this particular circumstance.

Parviz was happily inducted, stayed happy in the Army, and made many good friends there, but managed to look unhappy for a few hours every Thursday, when he was allowed to visit home. Haj Rahim's respect for me diminished considerably, I felt. He would not call me professor again, until I became one, years later.

"Sit down and fill out the questionnaire," ordered the corporal in charge, when I went to the Draft Registry to obtain my coveted exemption card. Hundreds of young men were applying for exemption on various grounds: inadequate health, family obligations as a result of being the only bread-winning male in the family, and of course lottery outcomes. I sat down and started on the printed form. On the line asking for "educational status," I proudly wrote "licentiate in mathematics and statistics." Giving my seat to another applicant, I stood up, placed the completed form on the corporal's desk, "upside down," as instructed sternly by him, and waited for him to process my exemption document. I allowed myself to bask in the pleasure of imminent freedom, though only theoretical for the moment, to go abroad and study.

"What is this?" asked the corporal, when he picked my form up and turned it to its front page with the authority of a school teacher perusing a pupil's homework. He was referring to my educational status. "It means," I explained patiently and respectfully, "that I have a higher degree from the university." He motioned to the multitude of exemption applicants waiting in line, and made it clear that I was wasting his valuable time by irrelevancies. "Look," he said, insisting on a clear answer before he finally stamped my card, "I don't care what degree you have or don't have. Pay attention and try to answer this very simple question: are you or are you not a diplomate?"

THE EDITOR-IN-CHIEF OF the Tabriz Voice had extra-ordinary news for me when I arrived in his office to submit my weekly contribution. "Mr. Director would like to meet you," he said. Mr. Director? Me? The unusually young editor, not quite twenty years old yet, but my senior by four years, was just as surprised as I was. In a few years he would move to Tehran, the capital city, and become a real editor of a real weekly, where he would actually earn a living, eventually to be rec-ognized as a popular novelist. For now he headed the group of unimportant employees working in the outer office. The only important person in the organization, the owner and publisher of the paper, occupied the inner office and was referred to as "Mr. Director" by everybody. The editor was "Javad Agha" to everyone in the office. That they called him by his first name Javad, followed and not preceded by the title of "Agha" – a postponed "Mr." that was more endearing than respectful – indicated that things were amicable in the outer office.

To enter or leave his own private room, Mr. Director had to go through the large outer office. Whenever he did so, all the employees rose to their feet in unison. Every seated visitor automatically followed suit. Mr. Director would take a quick look around, and unless he spotted somebody of consequence among the visitors, he wouldn't stop to chat with anyone except Javad Agha. But he seemed to enjoy the attention he received. His imposing figure and demeanor inspired a lot of awe and a bit of fear, because he was rumored to be carrying a concealed hand-gun with him at all times. Having long cultivated an image of fearless journalist in the service of the people, and now being recognized as a rather distinguished and influential member of the community as a result, he was naturally assumed to have unidentifiable sworn enemies. Thus he had come to possess a gun license, an extremely rare honor for a civilian indeed. Javad Agha once informed me in strict confidence that he had actually seen Mr. Director's gun.

"To His Excellency, Mr. Heydar Radjavi" read the handwritten address on the envelope that the editor handed to me, confirming the intention of Mr. Director to meet me. I was baffled. It was true that flowery titles of this sort had traditionally been, and still were with the much older generation, a dime a dozen in all Iranian correspondence, both formal and social. For example, a letter to my octogenarian father, a minor businessman in the Tabriz bazaar, also known to have some literary skills, written by one of his contemporaries, would invariably include such outrageously exaggerated openings as "Presented to the scholar of the highest rank, the greatest nobleman, the most honorable man of commerce, His Excellency, Mr. Haj Abbas Ali Agha Radjavi, may God forever preserve his blessed shadow over us all." The younger generation only combined "Excellency" with the minimal "Mr." (or its feminine equivalent with "Mrs." if the rare occasion ever called for it) when addressing, say, the school principal. But I definitely did not expect to be anywhere near my own excellency for another ten years or so.

I opened Mr. Director's letter. It wasn't a prank. The pleasure of meeting me was respectfully requested at 6:30 p.m., that very day. Honored, stunned, and anxious, I took a seat and tried to occupy myself with the various magazines and newspapers lying on the table. I could easily do this for the remaining hour and a half. In fact, this was a very pleasant aspect of my association with the Tabriz Voice. It was customary among editors of the press in Iran to exchange free copies of their periodicals. Javad Agha took aggressive advantage of this tradition and filled the outer office with the kind of printed matter that neither he nor his friends and acquaintances, including me, could afford to buy. My good friend and classmate Hussen and I visited the Voice outer office several times a week, almost every day after school, to catch up on our reading. We felt entitled to this privilege; after all, we were both regular contributors to the paper with no monetary compensation.

Concentration was not easy, but I tried. I started by scanning the local press, but soon switched to more interesting papers just arrived from Tehran. There were perhaps five or six papers published in Tabriz at the time, none of them daily, none of them very good. The Voice was not much better or much worse than the others. It sold very few copies and its main source of income was Government payments for publishing official legal notices. Tabriz, the home of the first printing press and the first modern school in the country, "the cradle of the Iranian constitutional movement" at the dawn of the century, had seen respectable and serious daily papers in the past. But the social and political turmoil of the preceding decades, starting with World War One, had, according to the grownups we trusted, resulted in this pitiful state of the press in our city. Almost all of the surviving journalists and writers of Tabriz had migrated to the Capital, where they could enjoy relative political freedom. One had to turn to Tehran dailies for domestic and world news and for sensational scandal reports; to Tehran weeklies for exciting serialized stories; and to Tehran monthlies for more high-brow stuff.

Hussen and I both had high aspirations about our future collaborations with the best of the press. For now, we were very proud of our contributions to the Voice: Hussen produced a social comment column and I wrote the book reviews. We were learning our trade by reading the Tehran periodicals, of course, and never doubted the value of our self-assigned mission to improve the image of the local press, if not the entire intellectual life of our city itself.

The big clock on the outer office wall said 6:30 now, but Mr. Director hadn't arrived yet. I started to worry about my curfew time. My father had a strict rule: I had to be home before dark every day. Knowing that the audience with the important man couldn't possibly last more than a few minutes, I figured that trouble at home could be avoided if Mr. Director showed up within the next fifteen minutes or so. Anticipation and worry was becoming more intolerable by the minute. Had I perhaps annoyed Mr. Director by saying something objectionable in my column? I asked myself. I hadn't forgotten that just the previous academic year, both Hussen and I had been reprimanded, officially and in writing, by our school principal because of a politically sensitive article in a little magazine published by a bunch of audacious students. Hussen and I were only junior members of the group. Yet the principal's letter, with copies sent to our parents, stated that political matters were no business of high school students, and warned us that any repetition of our misdemeanor would definitely result in tougher action by the school authorities. My father, always careful not to provoke the Establishment unnecessarily, was in total agreement with his Excellency the principal. It was because of this incident that I had started to use a pseudonym in all my further attempts at enlightening the reading public. But Mr. Director couldn't be really mad at me, I assured myself repeatedly, if he could address me as respectfully as he did on the envelope of his invitation note. Unless, of course, he was making fun of me.

Mr. Director appeared in the outer office, mercifully without much further delay. I participated in the collective ritual greeting by standing up, staying up while he passed through, and watching him disappear into the inner office after a quick, private chat with Javad Agha. The editor then motioned me to proceed, which I did nervously. What if this was a big mistake, and Mr. Director was under the impression that I was a grownup? Wouldn't he be disappointed to find that the columnist he had so respectfully addressed was a mere high school student? But as soon as I entered Mr. Director's fancy little office, he made all my fears evaporate. He got up and asked me to take a seat. He rang his bell to summon his servant from the outer office, and ordered the customary tea and sweets for the guest. He then leaned back on his luxurious desk chair and told me the reason for our meeting. "I wanted to personally congratulate you," he said, "on your most recent column." I didn't think my last column was so different from the previous ones, so why was he singling it out?

"Didn't you hear it on the radio yourself?" he asked, evidently surprised by the puzzled look on my face. "An excerpt from your book review column was read on Radio Tabriz yesterday," he was pleased to inform me. He reminded me that only one item was selected each week from one of the local papers to be read over the Government-run provincial radio. Why was my article chosen that week, instead of the usual samples of wisdom dispensed from the pens of safe, established, old men of the city? I wouldn't have a clue until a little later. For now I was very excited and happy to hear the news; I celebrated the occasion by helping myself, again and again, to the biscuits offered by Mr. Director. I didn't tell him that real radio sets were not allowed in my household and that the reception on my little crystal earphone radio was not always reliable. "I am very appreciative of your cooperation with us," Mr. Director said, as he rose to terminate the audience, "and I sincerely hope that your fruitful association with the Voice will continue even after your graduation from high school."

Walking home, I mentally examined my most recent book-review column that seemed to have started me up on the ladder of fame. It was a short but ambitious piece: I had produced a critique of a new translation of Franz

Kafka's *Metamorphosis,* no less. What made the effort even more remarkable was that the translation into Persian was done by two very prominent personages. One of the two was Sadegh Hedayat, who was, and still is, recognized by many scholars as the most important writer of twentieth-century Iran; certainly one of the most important according to almost everybody, including his political opponents then, and his fundamentalist enemies now. Some called him "Iran's own Kafka". My strongly negative piece was inspired by the books and periodicals, some of them underground, that I was reading at the time. "The present state of Persian literature is so utterly confused," reads the opening paragraph of my article in the yellowed pages of the Tabriz Voice, still in my possession today, "that absolutely anything goes, whether good or bad, useful or harmful." Kafka is denounced in the first paragraph as one of the leading representatives of "reclusive art," whose work has no redeeming value whatsoever. "Every main character in the story is pathetic," another scathing paragraph asserts, "and has nothing worthwhile to teach us." The review goes on to condemn the translators for their "long-winded effort" in the introduction of the book to make Kafka acceptable, and to lead the innocent readers astray.

The short essay was, as it is easy to see now, a transparent amalgam of the world-views of three distinct and often mutually opposing intellectual camps in mid-twentieth-century Iran. One consisted of the proponents of socialist realism, who had never quite forgiven Hedayat for abandoning their camp after a short period of flirtation, although they grudgingly acknowledged his prominence. A second camp belonged to the rationalist-pragmatist social and moral reformers who had little time for "useless" literature in general, and abhorred fiction and poetry altogether. According to them, reading "false" stories and "exaggerated" poetry was detrimental to the mental health of the nation. The third camp was that of religious literalists who didn't mind a fable so long as it had a discernible moral that encouraged pious behavior, but they detested writers like Hedayat for their open and unbounded irreverence.

How grateful I would feel, a few years later in college, toward my then late father for having saved me great future embarrassment by inadvertently making all propagation of my early opinions pseudonymous. For now, I increased my pace to make it home before dark, while basking in the glory of recognition. The unique radio station in the province was certainly more respectable and less provincial than the newspapers in Tabriz, I kept saying to myself. I knew also that, unlike the papers, Radio Tabriz actually paid people for their efforts. It paid its news announcers, musicians, and writers. Radio work was prestigious. Perhaps, I quietly hoped, I could use my new-found credentials to apply for a part-time position at the Radio. I daydreamed of the opportunity I would have to meet the glamorous Radio personalities, especially Treza Mangazarian, the young woman whose pure love songs I eagerly listened to on my toy radio, whom I had never seen in person or in a picture, and who would, I was certain, prove to be as beautiful as her songs.

I must tell somebody in my family, I decided as I approached home. Besides Hussen and those connected with the Voice, very few people knew who *H. R. Mehr*, this mysterious columnist so deservedly honored by Radio Tabriz, was. This wasn't fair. I knew I could not tell Father. Mother would be too worried about Father finding out if I told her. This left only one choice: my older brother, aged about thirty at the time, almost as cautious a man as Father was when it came to disturbing the Establishment. But I thought he would understand and would be proud of his kid brother; this was just a literary matter, anyway; and he himself had some association with Radio Tabriz, which had invited him on several occasions to recite classical poetry.

"Let me see the article," my brother demanded urgently, when I informed him of the happy news. No congratulatory notes were detectable in his reaction. I complied promptly and proudly. His face reddened as he went through my column. "Never, never, publish a thing like this again;" he admonished me, "don't you know what happens to authors of political articles like this?" He didn't allow me to protest. "Of course it is political;" he continued, guessing and countering my objection, "don't you see? You are taking sides with communists attacking their former fellow-travelers!" He ignored my protestations and just went on, "You think that you have made your own opinion and you think that this is only about literature. Let me tell you; this is dangerous stuff. Don't you remember how many university students were chased, injured, and put in jail by the police last year? All they did was participate in peace demonstrations; nothing political, right? Wrong! They were on the same side as communists about the peace issue! Why do you think your article was chosen by Radio Tabriz? Who do you think made the selection and read it over the Radio? No doubt a closet communist sympathizer, an employee of the Government radio station, who doesn't dare to voice his own opinions on these matters openly."

My brother made a deal with me: he wouldn't tell Father about my stupid and dangerous meddling in politics if I promised to stop right away. To scare me into sticking to my side of the deal, he reminded me of the hanging in public, a few years earlier, of a former school friend of his for political crimes. "Just like you," my brother recalled, "he started with this supposedly harmless literary criticism stuff when he was very young and inexperienced, but inevitably graduated to more political writings." But that happened four years ago, I thought, and things had surely started to change. Nobody would ever be hanged again for just expressing opinions. Couldn't my brother see all the newspapers coming from Tehran these days? Couldn't he hear how freely and loudly the Parliamentarians were now talking about nationalizing the Iranian oil industry and making the British pay a fair price for our oil? I pitied him for being too old to understand.

After allowing for a cooling-off period of several weeks, I resumed my column. I shouldn't be intimidated by the scared old folks, I decided, and writing under a brand new, completely unrecognizable pseudonym, I felt quite safe. My book-reviewing career would, however, be brought to an abrupt end soon, and unexpectedly; not by my father and brother, not by the school principal, and not by the police, but by the publication of a fake book.

One of the very few people who now knew the man behind my pen name was the old, kind, learned, and trustworthy owner and proprietor of a second-hand book store that Hussen and I frequented. "You didn't buy it from my store," he would say to us whenever he sold us a book arbitrarily banned by the Tabriz Police. He sold us inexpensive old books on religion, sociology, and politics. Hussen and I had come to like his religious outlook. He was so different from our elders: unlike them, he had no objections to reading books that "would plant seeds of doubt in the young minds and lead them astray." On the contrary, he encouraged such readings. "True faith can only come," he said, "after profound doubt." My friend and I didn't quite follow the logic, but if the old man had had profound doubts in the past, as was implied, and yet managed to be so serenely religious after all his years, that was good enough for us. We could now read all those doubt-spreading books without guilt or fear. His courage astounded us when he and his grand-son participated in unauthorized peace demonstrations that were violently met by the police. "Just because communists and atheists also demonstrate for peace," he said, "should I demonstrate for war?" Hussen and I wished our folks had minds half as broad as his.

The old man also dealt in bound periodicals. To make money for buying books, I occasionally bound journals for him. Hussen sold him some very old books, which his family had inherited and found useless. We both looked forward to our transactions and conversations with him, and we always brought him complimentary copies of the Tabriz Voice with our columns. He offered generous encouragement and mild criticism.

The bookseller broached the subject very delicately one afternoon. "It is of course no fault of the reviewer," he said, referring to my most recent column, "but we have to face the fact that there are charlatans out there, like this guy." The subject of my new review was a novel by Stefan Zweig in translation, and the old man was referring to the translator. Zweig was at the time one of the most widely translated Western writers in Iran. "You know," said the bookseller, himself a Zweig fan, "as I understand, poor Zweig wrote 52 books in his entire life. But guess how many of them have been translated into Persian." I couldn't guess. He smiled sadly, raised his eyebrows and, as gently as he could, informed me of the bad news: "54," he said. "And not everything he wrote has been translated either! No reflection on you the reviewer, as I said, but this fraud, like a few others before him, has taken advantage of the author's popularity. He has translated a book that Zweig never wrote."

ACKNOWLEDGMENTS

MY WIFE URSULA has read, proof-read, and made valuable comments and suggestions. She has never failed to smile or cry when reading a story even after the third time. Without her encouragement and persistent prodding these stories would not have been submitted for publication.

Our daughters Marjan, Shirin, and Carrie, who constituted the initial target audience for the stories, read them with sweet amazement and asked for more.

Many friends have shown interest and support. I only mention those few whose encouragement came very early, i.e., when I wrote the first three stories nine years ago. Peter Rosenthal, my long-time friend and mathematical coauthor, never stopped trying to convince me that it wasn't just because of our friendship that he liked the stories. Rebecca Lee Green read those first stories and offered kind, constructive criticism. Janez Bernik, Peter Fillmore, Keith Johnson, Leo Livshits, Gordon MacDonald, Matjaz Omladic, Chelluri Sastri, and Peter Semrl emboldened me to continue writing. Laurent Marcoux enthusiastically, and unilaterally, assumed the role of my unpaid publicist among my colleagues long before this book appeared on the horizon.

ABOUT THE AUTHOR

HEYDAR RADJAVI was born and raised in Tabriz and did not leave that city until he was admitted to the University of Tehran in 1953. He was in love with modern Persian literature and dreamed of being a writer until he switched to mathematics at the end of high school (but that is another story). He was sent to the University of Minnesota, where he got his doctorate in 1962. He then taught in Iranian, American, and Canadian universities until he moved permanently to Canada in 1972. He now resides in Waterloo, Ontario, with his wife Ursula. He has published books and articles in mathematical journals, and has been known to most of his friends and acquaintances as a mathematician. This collection constitutes his first publication outside mathematics in 55 years.

SOME OTHER MAGE TITLES

Garden of the Brave in War
Terence O'Donnell

Tales of Two Cities: A Persian Memoir
Abbas Milani

Crowning Anguish: Taj al-Saltana
Memoirs of a Persian Princess
Introduction by Abbas Amanat / Translated by Anna Vanzan

A Man of Many Worlds
The Diaries and Memoirs of Dr. Ghasem Ghani
Cyrus Ghani / Paul Sprachman

Stories from Iran: A Chicago Anthology 1921-1991
Edited by Heshmat Moayyad

Savushun: A Novel about Modern Iran
Simin Daneshvar / Translated by M.R. Ghanoonparvar

My Uncle Napoleon
Iraj Pezeshkzad / Translated by Dick Davis

Vis and Ramin
Fakhraddin Gorgani / Translated by Dick Davis

Shahnameh: the Persian Book of Kings
Abolqasem Ferdowsi / Translated by Dick Davis

Borrowed Ware: Medieval Persian Epigrams
Translated by Dick Davis

From Persia to Napa: Wine at the Persian Table
Najmieh Batmanglij

Silk Road Cooking: A Vegetarian Journey
Najmieh Batmanglij

*Food of Life: Ancient Persian and
Modern Iranian Cooking and Ceremonies*
Najmieh Batmanglij

*Happy Nowruz: Cooking with Children to Celebrate
the Persian New Year*
Najmieh Batmanglij

The Persian Garden: Echoes of Paradise
Mehdi Khansari / M. R. Moghtader / Minouch Yavari

*The Persian Sphinx:
Amir Abbas Hoveyda and the Iranian Revolution*
Abbas Milani

Masters and Masterpieces of Iranian Cinema
Hamid Dabashi

The Strangling of Persia
Morgan Shuster

The Persian Revolution of 1905–1909
Edward G. Browne / Introduction by Abbas Amanat

The History of Theater in Iran
Willem Floor

Agriculture in Qajar Iran
Willem Floor

Inside Iran: Women's Lives
Jane Howard

*Iran and the West
Volumes I & II*
Cyrus Ghani